Company's Coming

BARBECUES

Russ & Andrea
June 21, 1997
Wishing you the Lord's best
in all you do!
With all our love!
Pete, Bev, Mike, Brett & Mikayla
Alan, Pauline, Chelsey & Amy

Jean Paré

Dedication

If you can't stand the heat ... get out of the kitchen!

Cover Photo

BARBECUES

Twelfth Printing June 1997

ISBN 0-9693322-5-4

Published and Distributed by
Company's Coming Publishing Limited
Box 8037, Station "F"
Edmonton, Alberta, Canada
T6H 4N9

**Published Simultaneously in
Canada and the United States of America**

Printed In Canada

Company's Coming Cookbooks
by Jean Paré

table of Contents

the Jean Paré story

Jean Paré grew up understanding that the combination of family, friends and home cooking is the essence of a good life. From her mother she learned to appreciate good cooking, while her father praised even her earliest attempts. When she left home she took with her many acquired family recipes, her love of cooking and her intriguing desire to read recipe books like novels!

In 1963, when her four children had all reached school age, Jean volunteered to cater to the 50th anniversary of the Vermilion School of Agriculture, now Lakeland College. Working out of her home, Jean prepared a dinner for over 1000 people which launched a flourishing catering operation that continued for over eighteen years. During that time she was provided with countless opportunities to test new ideas with immediate feedback—resulting in empty plates and contented customers! Whether preparing cocktail sandwiches for a house party or serving a hot meal for 1500 people, Jean Paré earned a reputation for good food, courteous service and reasonable prices.

"Why don't you write a cookbook?" Time and again, as requests for her recipes mounted, Jean was asked that question. Jean's response was to team up with her son, Grant Lovig, in the fall of 1980 to form Company's Coming Publishing Limited. April 14, 1981, marked the debut of "150 DELICIOUS SQUARES", the first Company's Coming cookbook in what soon would become Canada's most popular cookbook series. By 1995, sales had surpassed ten million cookbooks.

Jean Paré's operation has grown from the early days of working out of a spare bedroom in her home to operating a large and fully equipped test kitchen in Vermilion, Alberta, near the home she and her husband Larry built. Full-time staff has grown steadily to include marketing personnel located in major cities across Canada plus selected U.S. markets. Home Office is located in Edmonton, Alberta where distribution, accounting and administration functions are headquartered in the company's own 20,000 square foot facility. Growth continues with the recent addition of the Recipe Factory, a 2700 square foot test kitchen and photography studio located in Edmonton.

Company's Coming cookbooks are now distributed throughout Canada and the United States plus numerous overseas markets, all under the guidance of Jean's daughter, Gail Lovig. The series is published in English and French, plus a Spanish language edition is available in Mexico. Familiar and trusted Company's Coming-style recipes are now available in a variety of formats in addition to the bestselling soft cover series.

Jean Paré's approach to cooking has always called for quick and easy recipes using everyday ingredients. She continues to gain new supporters by adhering to what she calls "the golden rule of cooking": never share a recipe you wouldn't use yourself. It's an approach that works—*ten million times over!*

Foreword

Barbecues have brought us full circle from the days of the caveman when cooking outdoors was a necessity, to cooking in modern indoor kitchen facilities, and back to the great outdoors!

Today, barbecuing provides a form of entertainment which is relaxed and casual. Complete or partial meals can be cooked outdoors where the cook is definitely one of the crowd. Think of your barbecue as an extra stove available to bake, roast, and grill food. Preparation is much the same, but clean-up is so easy. Cooking on the barbecue can be so versatile. Meat usually claims center stage of barbecue meals.

This book contains a lot more such as Barbecued Apple Pie, Bran Muffins, fresh bread, appetizers and desserts as well as salads that will complement your meal and can be prepared well ahead of time. Your guests will all want to help!

The more you barbecue, the more you will want to barbecue! The correct temperature for cooking is very important. Always preheat the barbecue for 15 minutes. A simple heat test for an open barbecue is to hold the palm of your hand close to the grill. If you can hold it there for 2 seconds it is hot; for three seconds it is medium hot; 4 seconds it is medium and 5 seconds it is low. Windy, rainy and cool weather will affect the length of cooking required. Cooking times given in this book are a guide only. Best results are achieved when cooking food which is at room temperature. If meat is chilled or slightly frozen it will take longer to reach the desired doneness.

A set of long handled barbecue utensils, a wire hamburger rack, a fish rack, pie irons, a meat thermometer, metal and wooden skewers, are wonderful extras to have on hand when barbecuing. Aluminum foil is a necessity. Use a "drugstore-wrap" when enclosing food, by bringing ends of foil up together, fold over one inch (2.5 cm) and keep folding until snug and flat against food. Turn ends over twice. Use tongs for turning meat on the grill. Do not pierce or salt meat until after it is cooked so that the delicious juices are not lost. Basting sauces containing sugar or tomato should only be used during the last five to ten minutes of cooking as they tend to burn easily.

Some people become very adept at cooking steak by looks or by touch. Cook steak on one side until juices come to the top. Turn and cook for approximately the same length of time. The steak will be rare and will feel very soft. For medium-doneness, cook on one side until top is covered with juice, turn and cook for approximately the same amount of time. The steak will fell slightly springy. For well-done steak, cook on each side until any juice that might appear is clear and the steak feels quite firm. Many people say never to turn steak more than once, while others say to turn often. This illustrates why the look and feel of the meat is important in determining the degree of doneness.

Outdoor appetites are hearty, so heat up the barbecue and start cooking.

Jean Paré

CHEESE STUFFED MUSHROOMS

Blue cheese in the stuffing gives just the right nip.

Large mushrooms	18	18
Butter or margarine	¼ cup	50 mL
Finely chopped onion	⅓ cup	75 mL
Mushroom stems, chopped		
Dry bread crumbs	½ cup	125 mL
Crumbled blue cheese	¼ cup	50 mL
Parsley flakes	1 tsp.	5 mL
Seasoned salt	¼ tsp.	1 mL
Grated medium Cheddar cheese, for garnish		

Gently twist stems from mushrooms. Reserve stems.

Melt butter in frying pan. Add onion and chopped stems. Sauté until onions are soft and clear. Remove from heat.

Add bread crumbs, blue cheese, parsley and seasoned salt. Stir. Stuff mushroom caps.

Put a few shreds of Cheddar cheese on top for color. Cook on medium grill until soft and hot, about 10 minutes. Makes 18.

Pictured on page 89.

SEAFOOD APPETIZER

Shrimp, scallops and fish in bacon make a delightful few bites.

Medium size shrimp, shelled and deveined	6	6
Scallops	6	6
Firm white fish fillets, cut in chunks	6	6
Bacon slices, cut in half crosswise	9	9
Mushroom caps	12	12

Wrap shrimp, scallops and fish chunks each in bacon. Onto each skewer (presoak wooden skewers 30 minutes) thread 1 mushroom cap followed by shrimp, scallop, fish chunk and second mushroom cap. Cook over medium-hot grill until fish is cooked and bacon is crisp about 10 minutes. Makes 6 appetizers.

STUFFED MUSHROOMS

It is hard to guess what the stuffing is. Showy and tasty.

Cooking oil	1 tbsp.	15 mL
Red pepper, finely chopped	1	1
Dry bread crumbs	1/2 cup	125 mL
Chopped chives	1 tbsp.	15 mL
Parsley flakes	1 tsp.	5 mL
Grated Parmesan cheese	2 tbsp.	30 mL
Salt, sprinkle		
Large mushrooms	24	24
Cooking oil		

Heat cooking oil in frying pan. Add red pepper. Sauté until soft, about 5 minutes. Remove from heat.

Stir in bread crumbs, chives, parsley, Parmesan cheese and salt.

Gently twist stems from mushrooms. Save stems for another purpose. Stuff mushroom caps with crumb filling. Brush mushrooms with cooking oil. Place on grill over medium heat until soft and heated through, about 10 minutes. Makes 24.

Pictured on page 89.

BARBECUED ORANGES

Served in the best style. A good start to breakfast.

Oranges, cut in half crosswise	4	4
Brown sugar	8 tsp.	40 mL
Grand Marnier or Cointreau (or 1/4 tsp., 1 mL, rum flavoring in 1 tbsp., 15 mL, water)	4 tsp.	20 mL

Remove seeds if any. Loosen orange segments but leave in position. Sprinkle each half with 1 tsp. (5 mL) brown sugar and 1/2 tsp. (2 mL) Grand Marnier. Wrap in double thickness foil squares, 2 halves per package. Cook on grill, cut side up, for about 8 minutes until hot. To serve, drizzle warm juice over top. Makes 4 servings of 2 orange halves each.

Pictured on page 71.

NACHOS

Pop these on the barbecue for a quick snack to ward off hunger while the serious barbecuing gets underway.

Packaged barbecued corn chips		
Grated Monterey Jack cheese	1¼ cups	300 mL
Grated mild or medium Cheddar cheese	1¼ cups	300 mL
Bacon slices, cooked and crumbled	6	6
Canned chopped green chilies, with juice	4 oz.	114 g
Green onions, sliced	3	3
Sour cream for dipping		

On 6 squares of foil put corn chips in 6 inch (15 cm) circles. Crowd chips together. You should see very little foil, if any, under chips. If you would rather, chips may be grouped all together on one large piece of foil.

Sprinkle each circle with next 5 ingredients divided among them. Place on grill over medium-low heat. Close lid. Heat until cheese is melted and nachos are hot. Watch closely as they burn easily.

Have sour cream handy for dipping. Makes 6 nachos.

Pictured on page 35.

POTATO SKINS

Prepare these ahead. A quick appetizer enjoyed by everyone.

Medium baking potatoes, baked and cooled	4	4
Butter or margarine, softened		
Sour cream for dipping		

Cut potatoes into 4 lengthwise sections. Remove most of the inside potato leaving shells about ¼ inch (6 mm) thick. Brush both sides with softened butter. Place on grill over medium heat. Brown both sides. For a crisper finish don't butter skin side. Cook butter side down first then turn and toast skin side until crisp.

Serve sour cream for dipping. Makes 4 servings.

SAUSAGE ROLLS

These sausages are encased in bread instead of pastry.

Skinless sausages, about 16 to a pound (454 g)	1 lb.	454 g
White bread slices, crusts removed	16	16
Prepared mustard	2 tsp.	10 mL
Butter or margarine, melted	1/4 cup	50 mL

In frying pan cook sausages browning all sides. Cool to handle.

Roll bread lightly with rolling pin to flatten. Spread bread with mustard. Roll each sausage in bread slice.

Brush rolls with melted butter. Toast very slowly on grill over low heat. It is easier to place on rack above grill so sausages can warm a bit before toasting. If heat is too high, bread will toast before sausage is hot. May be heated in microwave oven then toasted on medium grill. Makes 16.

Pictured on page 89.

HAM AND CHEESE ROLLS

When ham is rolled up with its best companions, cheese and mustard, it provides a tasty appetizer.

Prepared mustard		
Cooked square ham slices	6	6
Onion powder, sprinkle		
Process Cheddar cheese slices	6	6
Butter or margarine, melted	2 tbsp.	30 mL

Spread a little mustard on each ham slice. Sprinkle with onion powder. Top with a slice of cheese. Roll up and secure with 3 wooden picks.

Brush with melted butter. Cook on medium-hot greased grill. Turn and brush with butter often until ham shows signs of browning and cheese shows signs of melting. Cut into three pieces. Remove picks to serve. Makes 18 portions.

Pictured on page 89.

HAM TIDBITS

These are good hot or cold. Simple to make. Just spread ham slices with cheesy horseradish.

Cream cheese, softened	4 oz.	125 g
Horseradish	2 tsp.	10 mL
Cooked square ham slices	8	8
Butter or margarine, melted	2 tbsp.	30 mL

Blend cheese and horseradish together until soft and spreadable.

Spread mixture over ham slices. Roll up. Insert 3 toothpicks through each roll to secure. Space evenly. To serve cold, cut between toothpicks.

To serve hot, place on greased grill over medium-hot heat until browned, about 5 to 10 minutes. Brush with butter and turn often as it heats. Cut between toothpicks. Makes 24.

Pictured on page 89.

SAUSAGE STUFFED MUSHROOMS

A spicy meat stuffing.

Sausage meat (or use 4-5 small skinless sausages)	1/4 lb.	125 g
Dry bread crumbs	1 tbsp.	15 mL
Chili sauce	1 tbsp.	15 mL
Garlic powder	1/8 tsp.	0.5 mL
Onion powder	1/8 tsp.	0.5 mL
Italian seasoning	1/8 tsp.	0.5 mL
Medium mushrooms	12	12

Scramble-fry sausage meat in frying pan until cooked.

Add next 5 ingredients. Stir well.

Gently twist stems from mushrooms. Save stems for another purpose. Stuff caps with sausage mixture. Place directly on grill over medium heat. Cook until soft and hot, about 10 minutes. Makes 12.

Pictured on page 89.

BARBECUED GRAPEFRUIT

This will probably be the highlight of breakfast. The grapefruit seems to take on a new texture. The best.

Grapefruit, pink is best	3	3
Brown sugar	6 tbsp.	90 mL
Sherry (or alcohol-free sherry)	6 tbsp.	90 mL
Maraschino cherries for garnish	6	6

Cut grapefruit in half crosswise. Remove seeds. Loosen fruit sections from membrane. Put each grapefruit half on double thickness of foil. Sprinkle each half with 1 tbsp. (15 mL) brown sugar and 1 tbsp. (15 mL) sherry. If using white grapefruit use a bit more sugar. These are the minimum quantities for sugar and sherry. It is especially nice to double quantities so as to have more juice. Try it both ways to find your preference. Wrap. Place cut side up on medium grill. Cook for 10 to 12 minutes until quite warm.

To serve, place a cherry in the center and drizzle warm juice over top. Serves 6.

Pictured on page 71.

STEW PACKETS

Add a salad and dessert and your meal is complete.

Round steak, cut into small cubes	1³/₄ lbs.	800 g
Carrots, thinly sliced	6	6
Potatoes, peeled and cubed	6	6
Medium onions, sliced	3	3
Celery, thinly sliced	³/₄ cup	175 mL
Salt, sprinkle		
Pepper, sprinkle		
Condensed cream of mushroom soup	2 x 10 oz.	2 x 284 mL

On 6 double thickness squares of aluminum foil, divide steak cubes, sliced carrot, potato, onion and celery. Sprinkle with salt and pepper.

Divide soup over top. Wrap. Place on grill over low heat. Close lid. Cook without turning for 1 hour, then check. If not quite cooked, rewrap and cook for a few more minutes. Makes 6 servings.

BURGERS WITH SLICED ONION

These burgers hide slices of onion between two layers of meat.

Onion slices	6	6
Butter or margarine	2 tbsp.	30 mL
Ground beef	2 lbs.	1 kg
Hamburger buns, split and buttered	6	6

Use large enough onion so slices are close to bun size. Melt butter in frying pan. Sauté slices being careful when turning to keep slices intact. This step may be omitted if you prefer to use raw onion.

Shape meat into 12 thin patties. Place onion slice between 2 patties. Press edges to seal. Grill about 10 minutes per side over medium-hot heat until well done. If using raw onion, allow about 14 minutes per side.

Insert patties into buns. Have condiments nearby. Makes 6 onion-stuffed burgers.

SAVORY SHORT RIBS

Allow plenty of time to marinate these ribs for a flavorful meat.

TOMATO MARINADE		
Tomato sauce	7¹/₂ oz.	213 mL
Cider vinegar	¹/₂ cup	125 mL
Dry onion flakes	1 tbsp.	15 mL
Worcestershire sauce	2 tsp.	10 mL
Granulated sugar	1¹/₂ tbsp.	25 mL
Prepared mustard	1 tsp.	5 mL
Pepper	¹/₂ tsp.	2 mL
Chili powder	1 tsp.	5 mL
Garlic powder	¹/₄ tsp.	1 mL
Cooking oil	¹/₄ cup	50 mL
Beef short ribs	3 lbs.	1.35 kg

Tomato Marinade: Combine first 10 ingredients together in small bowl.

Put short ribs into shallow pan. Pour Tomato Marinade over top. Coat all pieces. Cover. Refrigerate for 8 hours or overnight. Bring meat to room temperature before cooking. Place ribs on grill over low heat. Close lid. Cook for 10 minutes. Turn. Cook 10 minutes more with lid closed. Cook until tender, basting and turning every 10 minutes. Total time about 45 minutes. Serves 4.

BARBECUED SHISH KEBABS

Try something different. If you have no skewers, throw out birthday hints in every direction.

KEBAB MARINADE

Soy sauce	²/₃ cup	150 mL
Granulated sugar	¼ cup	50 mL
Cooking oil	¼ cup	50 mL
Worcestershire sauce	2 tbsp.	30 mL
Garlic clove, minced	1	1
Red wine vinegar	3 tbsp.	50 mL
Pepper	¼ tsp.	1 mL
Beef sirloin or lamb steak, ½ inch (1.25 cm) thick	4 lbs.	1.8 kg
Whole mushrooms, stems removed	16-24	16-24
Canned whole onions	14 oz.	398 mL
Green peppers, cut in squares	2	2
Red peppers, cut in squares	2	2
Cherry tomatoes	16	16
Zucchini, sliced	1	1

Stir first 7 ingredients together in bowl with tight fitting lid.

Cut meat into 1 inch (2.5 cm) thick slices then into squares. Combine with marinade, cover and chill for a minimum of 30 minutes up to several hours. Shake bowl often.

Arrange meat on 8 or more skewers (presoak wooden skewers 30 minutes) with vegetables. Place over medium-hot grill, turning as necessary, about 20 minutes total time. Baste with marinade near end of cooking. If you prefer well done meat or if meat chunks are large, they may be partly precooked under broiler and chilled until needed. Serves 8.

Paré Pointer

He was on the outside looking in after pulling the wool over his wife's eyes — with the wrong yarn.

TERIYAKI BEEF KEBABS

These shish kebabs are tops.

Water	¹/₂ cup	125 mL
Soy sauce	¹/₂ cup	125 mL
Brown sugar, packed	¹/₃ cup	75 mL
Vinegar	2 tbsp.	30 mL
Cooking oil	2 tbsp.	30 mL
Ginger	¹/₂ tsp.	2 mL
Garlic powder (or 2 cloves, minced)	¹/₂ tsp.	2 mL
Pepper	¹/₄ tsp.	1 mL
Sirloin steak, 1 inch (2.5 cm) thick	1¹/₂ lbs.	700 g

Combine first 8 ingredients in deep bowl. Stir well.

Cut steak into 1 inch (2.5 cm) cubes. Add to mixture in bowl. Stir so all pieces are coated with sauce. Marinate for 1 hour at room temperature. Thread on skewers (presoak wooden skewers 30 minutes). Cook on medium-hot grill for a total time of about 14 minutes for medium. Baste often with sauce. Makes 4 servings.

1. Pineapple Beans page 142
2. Corn Muffins page 44
3. Mayonnaise Biscuits page 46
4. Barbecued Biscuit page 46
5. BBQ Baked Potatoes page 136
6. Grilled T-Bone page 21
   with Bush Fire Steak Sauce page 82
7. Vegetable Packets page 131
8. Onion Ring Special page 129
9. Boneless Short Ribs page 34
10. Java Ribs page 100

BARBECUED MEATLOAF

This flattish loaf is cooked on the grill. A good tasting loaf.

Lean ground beef	1½ lbs.	750 g
Finely chopped onion	⅓ cup	75 mL
Salt	1½ tsp.	7 mL
Pepper	¼ tsp.	1 mL
Chili sauce	1 cup	250 mL
Brown sugar, packed	¼ cup	50 mL
Vinegar	2 tbsp.	30 mL
Mustard powder	1 tsp.	5 mL
Drops of hot pepper sauce	3	3

In medium size bowl mix ground beef, onion, salt and pepper together well. Shape into a somewhat flattened loaf. Wrap in double thickness of foil. Cook over indirect medium heat (see page 149) with the lid down for about 1¼ hours.

Mix remaining ingredients together in bowl. Open foil. Spread sauce over top. Leave foil open. Close lid. Cook about 15 minutes more until bubbly. Serves 6.

Pictured on page 107.

CHEESE FILLED BURGERS

An inside-out cheeseburger.

Ground beef	1½ lbs.	680 g
Seasoned salt	1 tsp.	5 mL
Sweet pickle relish	4 tsp.	20 mL
Slices of medium Cheddar cheese	4	4
Hamburger buns, split, toasted if preferred and buttered (optional)	4	4

Mix ground beef and seasoned salt together. Divide into 8 equal balls. Flatten into 8 patties.

Spread relish on each of 4 patties keeping in from sides. Divide cheese among the same 4 patties. Cover with other patties. Press edges to seal. Cook on medium-hot grill, turning to cook other side about 10 minutes per side until well done.

Place meat in buns. Pass the condiments. Makes 4.

BEEF CUBES

You can serve individual kebabs or push off all meat cubes onto a bed of lettuce or onto a plain platter to serve. Extra good.

ONION SOUP MARINADE

Sherry (or alcohol-free sherry)	¹/₂ cup	125 mL
Soy sauce	¹/₂ cup	125 mL
Lemon juice	1 tbsp.	15 mL
Onion soup mix (envelope)	1	1
Brown sugar	2 tbsp.	30 mL
Cooking oil	2 tbsp.	30 mL
Beef steaks, cut in 1 inch (2.5 cm) cubes (sirloin is good)	2 lbs.	900 g

Onion Soup Marinade: Combine sherry, soy sauce, lemon juice, onion soup mix, brown sugar and cooking oil in deep bowl.

Add meat cubes. Let marinate for 3 to 4 hours in refrigerator. Thread meat on skewers (presoak wooden skewers 30 minutes). Cook on medium-hot grill for about 10 minutes. Turn. Baste with sauce. Grill for 10 minutes more for medium. Makes 6 servings.

GRILLED BEEF TENDERLOIN

The most tender steak of all.

Beef tenderloin	4¹/₂ lbs.	2 kg
Butter or margarine, melted	¹/₂ cup	125 mL
Powdered beef bouillon	1 tsp.	5 mL
Worcestershire sauce	2 tsp.	10 mL
Red wine vinegar	1 tbsp.	15 mL

Bend small end of tenderloin back so as to form a nice even roll. Tie securely.

Combine next four ingredients together and brush tenderloin with mixture. Since tenderloin is quite fat-free, brush with butter mixture often as you grill it. A meat thermometer will allow you to cook to desired degree of doneness. Sear all sides on hot grill. Continue to cook and baste over medium-hot heat. Serves 8 to 10.

GRILLED T-BONE

The choice of many for a special barbecue. Meat may be basted with cooking oil instead of the basting sauce or just barbecued plain and salted and peppered before eating. Bring on the hearty appetites.

T-bone steaks	4	4
BASTING SAUCE		
Steak sauce	2 tbsp.	30 mL
Basil	$1/2$ tsp.	2 mL
Water	2 tbsp.	30 mL

Have steaks at room temperature. Trim off most of the fat. Cook on medium-hot grill, about 7 minutes per side for medium. A steak that is 2 inches (5 cm) thick will need about 25 to 30 minutes total.

Basting Sauce: Mix steak sauce, basil and water together. As steak nears doneness, brush with sauce several times. Serves 4.

PORTERHOUSE STEAK: A larger steak than the T-bone, porterhouse steak contains more of the tenderloin. Grill the same as for T-bone. If dividing steaks be sure to include a section of the loin with each serving.

HOT T-BONE: Barbecue steaks plain then spoon Bushfire Steak Sauce, page 82, over top of each.

Pictured on page 17.

ROAST MEAT AND POULTRY

It is very simple to use your barbecue as an oven. Keep the heat outside.

Roast of beef, pork or other meat or use chicken, turkey or other poultry

Place meat in covered roaster (or uncovered if you prefer). Heat barbecue with lid closed. It is best to place an oven thermometer inside until you get to know your barbecue. Usually when set on low, the inside temperature will be about 325° to 350°F (160° to 180°C). When set on medium the inside temperature will be about 400°F (200°C). For most roasts and poultry set heat on low. Put roaster on grill in heated closed barbecue. Proceed to cook as in your indoor oven. Allow about the same cooking time.

SIRLOIN GRILL

This is the easiest of the tender steaks to cut into portions. Also the most economical.

Sirloin steaks, about 1 inch **(2.5 cm) thick**	**4 lbs.**	**1.8 kg**
Cooking oil		

Barbecue Sauce, see page 84
  (optional)

Butter or margarine (optional)

Bring steaks to room temperature. Slash fat edges to ensure steaks will not curl but will lie flat. Trim off excess fat to avoid flare up. Rub lightly with cooking oil. Place steaks on medium-hot grill. Cook for about 7 minutes per side for medium.

As meat nears doneness, baste with barbecue sauce if desired. When meat is turned, sprinkle cooked side with salt & pepper.

Just as you serve each piece of steak, put a dab of butter on top. It will add a special touch. Serves 5 to 6.

RIB EYE STEAKS

These are also known as Delmonico Steaks. Tender and succulent.

Rib eye steaks, 1 inch (2.5 cm) thick	**6**	**6**
Cooking oil		

Maître D'Hôtel Butter, see page 83

Cook on medium-hot grill, about 10 minutes per side for medium. Brush with cooking oil occasionally as it cooks.

Place a coin of Maître D'Hôtel Butter on each steak as you serve it. Serves 6.

BEEF ON A BUN: Thicker steaks thinly sliced make a very good filling in buttered hamburger buns. Pass mustard and ketchup, salt and pepper.

PEPPER STEAK

Crushed peppercorns are pushed into this steak with your hand. Not nearly as pepper-hot as you would think.

Black peppercorns	3 tbsp.	50 mL
Servings of sirloin steak	6	6
Cooking oil (optional)		
Salt, sprinkle		
Butter or margarine pats	6	6

Put peppercorns in a plastic bag. Crush, using meat mallet or a hammer. Using the heel of your hand push crushed peppercorns into both sides of meat using more if needed.

Cook on greased medium-hot grill about 7 minutes per side for medium. If steak is less than 1 inch (2.5 cm) thick it will take a bit less time. Baste with cooking oil if desired. Some pepper may be scraped off if you wish before serving or serve as is. It is super just as is.

Sprinkle with salt. Place a pat of butter on each steak to serve. Serves 6.

SALISBURY STEAKS

A steak that's easy to sink your teeth into.

Eggs	2	2
Milk	1/4 cup	50 mL
Chopped onion	1/2 cup	125 mL
Rolled oats	1 cup	250 mL
Canned diced green chilies	1/4 cup	50 mL
Chili powder	1 tsp.	5 mL
Salt	1 tsp.	5 mL
Pepper	1/4 tsp.	1 mL
Garlic powder	1/4 tsp.	1 mL
Ground beef	2 lbs.	1 kg

Beat eggs with spoon in large mixing bowl. Add next 8 ingredients. Stir.

Add ground beef. Mix well. Shape into 6 or 8 small steak-shape patties, about 1/2 inch (12 mm) thick. Pick up carefully and place on greased grill over medium-hot heat or cook in wire basket. Cook for about 10 minutes per side until well done. Makes 6 to 8 servings.

TOURNEDOS

Always tender, these fat-free steaks need basting with butter or cooking oil.

Filet steaks	4	4
Bacon slices	4	4
Butter or margarine, melted	3 tbsp.	50 mL
Salt, sprinkle		
Pepper, sprinkle		

Wrap each steak with bacon. Secure with pick. Brush with melted butter. Sear on hot grill to brown. Turn. Brush again with butter. Total cooking time, about 10 to 12 minutes. Before serving brush with butter once more. Sprinkle with salt and pepper. Serves 4.

Note: If butter causes too much smoking, baste with cooking oil instead.

FILET MIGNON: Omit bacon slices. Brush with butter or margarine several times.

BLADE STEAK

An economical steak that shouldn't be overlooked.

Blade steak, ³/₄ inch (2 cm) thick	1	1
Meat tenderizer, unseasoned		
Barbecue Sauce (optional) see page 84		

Sprinkle steak with meat tenderizer. Pierce all over with fork. Turn steak and repeat. Let stand at room temperature 30 minutes. Grill over medium-high heat for about 7 minutes per side for medium. Steak may be cut for easier turning.

Baste with barbecue sauce toward end of cooking time if desired.

CHUCK STEAK: Prepare and cook the same way as for blade. If cooking several chuck steaks it is best to remove top strip and use for stew meat. This top strip is the least tender of the steak.

ROUND STEAK BARBECUE

You can't go wrong with this marinade. While meat starts to cook, the marinade is thickened for the final basting.

FAVORITE MARINADE

Soy sauce	1/2 cup	125 mL
Sherry (or use red wine vinegar)	1/2 cup	125 mL
Vinegar	3 tbsp.	50 mL
Cooking oil	2 tbsp.	30 mL
Granulated sugar	2 tbsp.	30 mL
Ginger	1/2 tsp.	2 mL
Garlic powder	1/4 tsp.	1 mL
Pepper	1/4 tsp.	1 mL
Round steak (or sirloin), 3/4 inch (2 cm) thick	1 1/2 lbs.	700 g
Cornstarch	1 tbsp.	15 mL
Water	2 tbsp.	30 mL

Favorite Marinade: Combine first 8 ingredients in small bowl. Stir well. Put into plastic bag.

Cut steak into serving size pieces. Add to marinade in plastic bag. Let marinate in sealed bag in refrigerator about 18 to 20 hours, or at least overnight. Cook on medium-hot grill, about 7 to 8 minutes per side for medium.

Pour marinade into small saucepan. Stir cornstarch into water. Add to marinade. Heat and stir over medium heat until it boils and thickens. Baste meat often during last part of cooking. Serves 4.

BARBECUED STEAKS

Most popular barbecue of all. So easy to give a different twist.

Sirloin steak	5 1/2 lbs.	2.5 kg

Horseradish Butter, page 82

Thaw steak if frozen. Place steak on medium-hot grill. Cook for about 7 minutes per side for medium.

Top with a coin of Horseradish Butter. Sprinkle with salt and pepper. Serves 8.

BARBECUED FLANK STEAK

If you are lucky enough to have any left, it makes an excellent cold sandwich. When sliced this meat is pink with a dark crusty edge all around.

Condensed beef consommé	2 x 10 oz.	2 x 284 mL
Soy sauce	$^2/_3$ cup	150 mL
Sliced green onions	$^1/_2$ cup	125 mL
Lemon juice	6 tbsp.	100 mL
Brown sugar, packed	$^1/_4$ cup	60 mL
Seasoned salt	1 tbsp.	15 mL
Garlic clove, minced	1	1
Large flank steaks	2	2
Beer	2 cups	500 mL

Mix first 7 ingredients together well.

Score steak in diamond pattern on both sides. Place in single layer in shallow pan. Pour consommé mixture over meat.

Without stirring, pour beer over top. Do not stir. Cover. Marinate for 24 hours in refrigerator. When ready to use, place meat on barbecue over medium-hot grill. Pour marinade into saucepan to heat while meat is cooking. Barbecue meat to desired doneness, about 6 minutes per side for rare. To serve, slice thinly against the grain in a sloped direction making slices wider than if sliced straight up and down. Serve with hot marinade. Makes about 4 servings.

MINUTE STEAK

Ever so quick!

Minute steaks	6	6
Cooking oil	$^1/_4$ cup	50 mL
Prepared mustard	2 tsp.	10 mL

Have steaks at room temperature.

Mix cooking oil and mustard together in small bowl or cup. Brush over meat on both sides. Cook on hot grill for about 2 minutes per side for medium. When grill has been taken up with lots of corn or other vegetables, this makes a fast finish to the meal. If you don't care for mustard brush with cooking oil only. Makes 6 servings.

TERIYAKI ROUND STEAK

A flavorful marinade for an economy cut of steak.

TERIYAKI MARINADE

Soy sauce	$^2/_3$ cup	150 mL
Brown sugar, packed	$^1/_2$ cup	125 mL
Sherry (or alcohol-free sherry)	$^1/_4$ cup	50 mL
Cooking oil	2 tbsp.	30 mL
Ginger	1 tsp.	5 mL
Garlic clove, minced	1	1
Seasoned salt	$^1/_2$ tsp.	2 mL
Round steak (or rump steak)	$3^1/_3$ lbs.	1.5 kg
Unseasoned meat tenderizer		

Teriyaki Marinade: Combine first 8 ingredients in deep bowl. Stir well.

Sprinkle steak with tenderizer. Poke holes all over with fork. Turn and repeat. Let stand for 30 minutes. Cut steak into serving size pieces. Add to bowl. Cover and marinate in refrigerator for 2 days. Before cooking let stand at room temperature for $^1/_2$ hour. Cook on medium-hot grill, brushing with marinade and turning occasionally, about 7 minutes per side for medium. Serves 6.

BRAN BURGERS

Bran makes a different addition to ground beef. Tasty.

Ground beef	2 lbs.	1 kg
All bran cereal	$^1/_2$ cup	125 mL
Sour cream	$^1/_2$ cup	125 mL
Finely chopped onion	$^3/_4$ cup	175 mL
Beef bouillon powder	$^1/_2$ tsp.	2 mL
Salt	2 tsp.	10 mL
Milk	$^1/_4$ cup	50 mL
Hamburger buns, split, toasted if preferred and buttered (optional)	10-12	10-12

Mix first 7 ingredients together in large bowl. Shape into 10 to 12 patties. Cook on grill over medium-hot heat for about 10 minutes per side until well done.

Serve meat in buns or as meat for main course. Have condiments ready for burgers. Makes 10 to 12 hamburgers.

PIT BARBECUE

An excellent way to serve a crowd. Be sure to read directions completely before beginning so you can be all ready to carry through smoothly from start to finish. Meat quantity may be increased or decreased as needed.

**Large boned and rolled round beef
roasts, allowing about $^1/_2$ lb. (225 g)
per person**

**Wide foil to wrap meat
Wire to go around roast and make handle
for easy removal
Stick with hook on end to lower and
remove meat
Tub to transport meat
Shovels for pit
Plywood and sticks for pit cover
Wood
Kindling
Newspaper
Steel tray with 2-3 inch (6-7.5 cm)
sides, with heavy wire attached
to corners**

Ask for a boned and rolled outside round roast and a boned and rolled inside round roast. The outside roast will be long and evenly rounded and will weigh from 15 to 20 lbs. (6.8 to 9 kg). The inside roast will be shorter, tapered a bit at the ends and the middle will be bigger around. It will weigh about 10 to 12 lbs. (4.5 to 5.5 kg).

Roasts can be cut in half for easier wrapping and handling. Wrap in double thickness of foil. Wrap wire around meat, using part of it to fashion a handle at top. Hook can then slip into this handle to raise and lower meat.

If desired, seasonings such as salt, pepper, garlic powder and onion powder, may be rubbed into surface of meat before wrapping.

Dig a pit 2 feet (.66 m) longer and wider than tray and 5 feet (1.6 m) deep.

You will need lots of wood. Fill pit with wood by layering in one direction first then criss-crossing each layer so it will breathe. Place several crumpled sheets of newspaper onto center of wood near ground level. Cover top and sides with lots of kindling. Continue piling wood to make a stack as high as you can reach and as big around as the pit.

(continued on next page)

Light the fire about 2 hours before you are ready to start cooking the meat. As the fire burns, embers will fall into the pit. There should be no flame left but lots of glowing embers. Place a few pounds of meat on tray. Lower into pit to rest over embers. Using hook on a stick lower rest of meat to tray.

Put lengths of wood 2 by 4 inch (6 by 12 cm) across hole, 2 feet (.6 m) apart.

Cover sticks with plywood, extending plywood beyond edges of pit. Cover plywood with thin layer of dirt about 2 to 3 inches (6 to 7.5 cm). Watch for escaping smoke or steam. If you see any, cover spot with more dirt. Allow meat to remain in pit for about 8 to 10 hours.

Remove dirt from plywood. Remove plywood and cross-sticks. Using hook, lift meat and put into a metal tub. Carry to the meal site and prepare to carve.

Note: Pork or lamb may be used instead of beef if you prefer.

SHORT RIBS

Grand choice for beef ribs. Ribs are pre-cooked ahead of time so it doesn't take much time to finish them off. Scrumptious.

Beef short ribs	**4 lbs.**	**1.8 kg**
Water to cover		
RIB MARINADE		
Ketchup	**1 cup**	**250 mL**
Cider vinegar	**3 tbsp.**	**50 mL**
Garlic powder (or 1 clove, minced)	**$1/4$ tsp.**	**1 mL**
Finely chopped onion	**$1/4$ cup**	**60 mL**
Prepared mustard	**2 tsp.**	**10 mL**
Pepper	**$1/2$ tsp.**	**2 mL**

Cover short ribs with water in large pot. Simmer covered for about 1 hour until tender. Drain. Transfer to large bowl.

Rib Marinade: Combine all 6 ingredients together in small bowl. Pour over short ribs. Be sure to coat each piece. Let stand 30 minutes. Place meat on greased grill over medium heat. Turn and baste occasionally for 20 to 30 minutes. Serves 4 to 6.

SAVORY ROUND STEAK

A grand marinade gives this a great flavor.

PIQUANT MARINADE		
Red wine vinegar	¹/₂ cup	125 mL
Soy sauce	¹/₄ cup	50 mL
Garlic clove, minced	1	1
Worcestershire sauce	2 tbsp.	30 mL
Prepared mustard	2 tbsp.	30 mL
Cooking oil	¹/₂ cup	125 mL
Round steak, ³/₄ inch (2 cm) thick	2¹/₂ lbs.	1 kg
Meat tenderizer, unseasoned		

Piquant Marinade: Combine first 6 ingredients in bowl. Stir.

Sprinkle 1 side of meat with tenderizer. Poke deep holes all over with fork. Turn and repeat on other side. Let stand for 30 minutes. Cut steak into serving size pieces. Add to marinade. Let stand several hours or overnight. Cook over medium-hot heat until done, about 15 minutes total time for medium. Serves 4 to 5.

SATAY

A sure-fire hit for a main course or an appetizer.

Sirloin steak, 1¹/₂ - 2 inches (4-5 cm) thick	1¹/₂ lbs.	750 g
SATAY MARINADE		
Soy sauce	²/₃ cup	150 mL
Granulated sugar	¹/₃ cup	75 mL
Ketchup	2 tbsp.	30 mL
Cooking oil	2 tbsp.	30 mL
Ginger powder	¹/₂ tsp.	2 mL
Garlic powder	¹/₄ tsp.	1 mL
Onion powder	¹/₄ tsp.	1 mL

Slice steak making long thin slices. This is much easier to do if meat is partially frozen. Presoak wooden skewers in water for 30 minutes.

(continued on next page)

Satay Marinade: In bowl that has a tight-fitting cover mix soy sauce, sugar, ketchup, cooking oil, ginger, garlic powder and onion powder. Stir well. Add meat strips pressing down to cover with sauce. Cover bowl. Marinate for $1/2$ to 1 hour or longer if you want to prepare well ahead of time. Turn bowl occasionally.

Thread meat strips on skewers accordion fashion. Lay on a tray. Transfer skewers to hot grill. Cook turning occasionally for about 4 to 5 minutes for well done. Makes 3 servings for main course and 6 as an appetizer.

Pictured on page 89.

GINGER BEEF

This tantalizing dish can be prepared in a wok or a large skillet. Serve with rice.

GINGER MARINADE

Soy sauce	3 tbsp.	50 mL
Oyster sauce	2 tbsp.	30 mL
Finely chopped ginger	$1^1/2$ tbsp.	25 mL
Sherry (or alcohol-free sherry)	2 tbsp.	30 mL
Cornstarch	1 tbsp.	15 mL
Granulated sugar	1 tsp.	5 mL
Salt	$1/2$ tsp.	2 mL
Sirloin or flank steak, cut in large matchsticks	1 lb.	454 g
Cooking oil	2 tbsp.	30 mL
Bok choy, cut in short strips	2 cups	500 mL
Frozen snow peas, thawed	6 oz.	170 g
Green onions, sliced	4	4

Ginger Marinade: Combine first 7 ingredients in deep bowl. Stir well.

Add meat. Marinate for 30 minutes.

Heat cooking oil in wok over hot grill. Remove meat from marinade and add to wok. Stir-fry for 4 minutes.

Add bok choy, snow peas and onion. Stir-fry until tender crisp, about 6 minutes. Serves 2.

Note: This is easy to double. After making second batch, add the first batch to wok. Heat and stir until hot.

CLUB STEAK

Just the right size for single servings.

CLUB MARINADE

Soy sauce	²/₃ cup	150 mL
Cooking oil	¹/₃ cup	75 mL
Cider vinegar	¹/₄ cup	50 mL
Lemon juice	¹/₄ cup	50 mL
Pepper	1 tsp.	5 mL
Garlic powder (or 2 cloves, minced) optional	¹/₂ tsp.	2 mL
Club steaks, about 1 inch (2.5 cm) thick	6	6

Marinade: Combine first 6 ingredients in small bowl.

Trim excess fat from meat. Slash fat to avoid curling. Put steaks into bowl and cover with marinade. Cover bowl. Chill for 6 to 8 hours. Bring meat to room temperature. Cook on greased grill over medium-high heat. For medium, cook about 7 minutes per side. Serves 6.

Variation: These steaks may be cooked without using marinade. As each side is cooked, sprinkle with salt and pepper. Brush with barbecue sauce occasionally as it cooks, if you like.

Note: To make even more tender, sprinkle 1 side with unseasoned meat tenderizer. Pierce all over with fork. Turn and do other side. Let stand 30 minutes. May be grilled now or marinated.

MUSTARD STEAK

About the most simple marinade there is. A bit of zip.

Prepared mustard	1 tbsp.	15 mL
Salad oil	1 tbsp.	15 mL
Sirloin steak, ³/₄ inch (2 cm) thick	2¹/₂ lbs.	1.14 kg

Stir mustard and salad oil together until smooth.

Brush both sides of steak with mustard mixture. Let stand at room temperature 30 minutes. Cook on medium-high grill until degree of doneness is reached, about 7 minutes per side for medium. Serves 4 to 5.

Just the right finishing touch for this tender steak.

Filet steaks	6	6
Cooking oil		
Blue cheese, softened	1/4 cup	50 mL
Butter or margarine, softened	1/2 cup	125 mL

Brush steaks lightly with cooking oil. Sear meat. Grill over medium-high heat until cooked, about 6 to 7 minutes per side for medium.

Mash cheese and butter together. Serve steaks with cheese mixture spread over top. Serves 6.

Hamburger with stuffing inside makes a good change of pace.

Dry bread crumbs	2/3 cup	150 mL
Dry onion flakes	2 tsp.	10 mL
Parsley flakes	1/2 tsp.	2 mL
Poultry seasoning	1/4 tsp.	1 mL
Salt	1/8 tsp.	0.5 mL
Pepper, light sprinkle		
Worcestershire sauce	1/2 tsp.	2 mL
Water	2 tbsp.	30 mL
Ground beef	2 lbs.	1 kg
Salt	1 tsp.	5 mL
Pepper	1/8 tsp.	0.5 mL

Measure first 7 ingredients into mixing bowl. Stir. Add water. Mix. Mixture should hold together when squeezed.

Put ground beef into a separate bowl. Sprinkle with second amount of salt and pepper. Mix well. Divide into 12 equal balls. Flatten into patties. Divide crumb mixture among 6 patties, placing in center and keeping back from edges. Cover with remaining patties. Press edges to seal. Cook on medium-hot grill for about 10 minutes per side, until well done. Makes 6 servings.

BONELESS SHORT RIBS

Start preparation the day before. It takes but a few minutes to sprinkle with tenderizer and refrigerate. An all meat short rib.

Beef short ribs	3 lbs.	1.35 kg
Meat tenderizer, unseasoned		
Pineapple juice	1¼ cups	300 mL
Soy sauce	¼ cup	50 mL
Brown sugar	1 tbsp.	15 mL
Ginger	¼ tsp.	1 mL

Cut meat from bones. Cut off fat. Sprinkle with tenderizer. Pierce all over with fork. Repeat on other side. Place on plate or plates in single layer. Cover. Put into refrigerator overnight.

In pan large enough to hold meat in single layer, mix pineapple juice, soy sauce, sugar and ginger. Add meat. Turn to coat. Return to refrigerator for about 5 hours. Turn occasionally. Remove meat and place over medium grill. Baste with sauce. Turn. Baste. Cook until browned turning and basting occasionally, about 20 to 25 minutes total time until tender. Makes 4 servings.

Pictured on page 17.

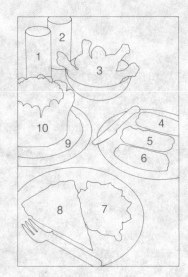

PIZZA BURGERS

These patties are served on French bread. Add vegetables and a salad for a super meal.

Lean ground beef	1 lb.	454 g
Dry bread crumbs	$^1/_3$ cup	75 mL
Finely chopped onion	$^1/_3$ cup	75 mL
Grated Parmesan cheese	$^1/_4$ cup	50 mL
Tomato paste	$5^1/_2$ oz.	156 mL
Salt	1 tsp.	5 mL
Pepper	$^1/_4$ tsp.	1 mL
Oregano	$^1/_2$ tsp.	2 mL
Mozzarella slices	6	6
Tomato slices	6	6
Mushroom slices	24	24
Green pepper, diced pieces	30	30
Grated medium Cheddar cheese	6 tbsp.	100 mL
French bread slices, toasted and buttered	6	6

In medium bowl combine first 8 ingredients. Mix together well. Shape into 6 slightly oval shaped patties. Cook on medium-hot greased grill, about 10 minutes per side until well done.

When meat is cooked put slice of mozzarella cheese on each patty followed by slice of tomato, 4 mushroom slices and 5 green pepper pieces. Sprinkle Cheddar cheese in center.

Serve each patty on a toasted and buttered slice of French bread. Makes 6 servings.

She wears her wedding ring on the wrong finger because she married the wrong man.

STIR-FRY MEAL

A quick meal with a good flavor. If your wok has handles that aren't heat-proof, use a large skillet.

Cooking oil	3 tbsp.	50 mL
Sirloin steak, cut in very thin slices	1 lb.	454 g
Sliced mushrooms	2 cups	500 mL
Sliced onion	2 cups	500 mL
Sliced celery	2 cups	500 mL
Green onions, sliced	10-12	10-12
Canned bamboo shoots, drained, cut in matchsticks	10 oz.	284 mL
Small red pepper, cut in matchsticks	1	1
Canned spinach, drained and chopped	1/2 cup	125 mL
Soy sauce	1/4 cup	50 mL
Granulated sugar	2 tsp.	10 mL
Beef bouillon powder	1 tsp.	5 mL
Hot water	1/2 cup	125 mL

Heat cooking oil in wok on grill over medium heat. Add steak pieces. Sauté until browned.

Add next 6 ingredients. Stir. Cover. Cook for 5 minutes.

Add spinach, soy sauce and sugar. Stir.

Dissolve beef bouillon powder in hot water. Add to wok. Stir-fry until tender, about 10 to 15 minutes. Makes 3 servings.

BETTER BURGERS

An old simple trick to get tasty meat with dry onion soup mix as the flavorful addition.

Ground beef	2 lbs.	900 g
Water	3/4 cup	175 mL
Envelope dry onion soup	1	1
Dry bread crumbs	1/3 cup	75 mL
Hamburger buns, split and buttered	10	10
Lettuce leaves	10	10
Onion slices	10	10
Tomato slices	10	10

(continued on next page)

In medium bowl mix ground beef with water.

Add soup mix and bread crumbs. Mix together well. Shape meat into 10 patties. Cook on greased medium-hot grill, about 10 minutes per side until well done.

Place lettuce on bun. Add onion and tomato. Lay hamburger patty over tomato. Have relish and ketchup on hand. Cover with top of bun. Makes 10 servings.

Pictured on page 53.

HAMBURGER PATTIES: Omit buns. Serve patties as meat for the meal.

HAMBURGERS

Everybody's favorite anytime. An all meat burger.

Ground beef	2 lbs.	1 kg
Worcestershire sauce	2 tbsp.	30 mL
Salt	1 1/2 tsp.	7 mL
Pepper	1/4 tsp.	1 mL
Hamburger buns, split, toasted if preferred and buttered (optional)	10	10

Mix first 4 ingredients together well. Shape into 10 patties or less depending on the size you prefer. A good average is 5 patties per pound (454 g). Grill about 10 minutes per side over medium-hot heat until well done. Add one or more of the trimmings from the condiment tray.

Place meat patties in buns. Pass the condiments. Makes 10.

Note: Ground beef with some fat in it produces a softer patty than extra lean hamburger.

CHEESEBURGER: After turning meat patties over, cook until nearly done. Lay a cheese slice over each patty. It will melt as meat finishes cooking.

CONDIMENT TRAY: Some popular items to serve can be nicely arranged on a large tray such as: cheese slices, slices of onion or chopped onion which may be raw or cooked, tomato slices, pickles, ketchup, mustard, sweet pickle relish, and lettuce.

MEATBALL SKEWERS

These may be served as a main course or just serve meatballs alone for an appetizer.

Butter or margarine	1 tbsp.	15 mL
Finely chopped onion	1/3 cup	75 mL
Egg white	1	1
Paprika	1 tsp.	5 mL
Salt	3/4 tsp.	4 mL
Pepper	1/8 tsp.	0.5 mL
Garlic powder	1/8 tsp.	0.5 mL
Lean ground beef	1 lb.	454 g
Onion chunks, 3-4 layers each	40	40
Cherry tomatoes	40	40
Mushroom caps	40	40
Cooking oil		

Melt butter in frying pan. Add onion. Sauté until soft. Cool.

In large bowl beat egg white, paprika, salt, pepper and garlic powder together lightly until blended. Add onion.

Add ground beef. Mix. Shape into 1 inch (2.5 cm) balls.

Thread onto skewers (presoak wooden skewers 30 minutes) alternating with vegetables. Cook on medium-hot grill turning often until well done, about 20 minutes total cooking time.

Brush with cooking oil occasionally. Makes 40 meatballs. Makes 4 servings as main course or 8 to 9 as an appetizer.

Pictured on page 125.

When you throw a zero up in the air you have a Flying None.

If your meat counter doesn't have thick sirloin steak just cut meat into squares.

Sirloin steak, 1¹/₂ inch (4 cm) thick	2 lbs.	900 g
BASTING SAUCE		
Ketchup	¹/₃ cup	75 mL
Cider vinegar	¹/₄ cup	50 mL
Soy sauce	2 tbsp.	30 mL
Molasses	2 tbsp.	30 mL

Cut meat into 1¹/₂ inch (4 cm) thick cubes. Thread on short skewers (presoak wooden skewers 30 minutes), 4 cubes each.

Basting Sauce: Combine all ingredients together. Cook meat skewers on medium-hot greased grill. Towards the end of cooking time baste often. Total cooking time, about 20 minutes for medium. Allow 2 skewers per person. Serves 5 to 6.

SIMPLE BEEF KEBABS: As meat is cooking brush several times with your favorite barbecue sauce or simply baste with cooking oil.

CHERRY COOLER

So pretty. A deep cherry pink color with a very pleasant cherry flavor.

Cherry flavored gelatin powder, 4 serving size	1	1
Hot water	2 cups	450 mL
Granulated sugar	¹/₄ cup	50 mL
Salt	¹/₈ tsp.	0.5 mL
Cold water	3 cups	700 mL
Lemon juice	¹/₃ cup	75 mL
Ginger ale	2 cups	450 mL

Dissolve gelatin in hot water in pitcher.

Add sugar and salt. Stir to dissolve. Add cold water and lemon juice. Chill.

Just before serving add ginger ale. Pour over ice cubes in tall glasses. Makes 7¹/₂ cups (1.7 L).

Pictured on page 35.

ORANGEADE

How long has it been since you have had old-fashioned orangeade?

Water	4 cups	900 mL
Granulated sugar	1/2 cup	125 mL
Juice of oranges	4	4
Juice of lemon	1	1

Put water and sugar in pitcher. Stir to dissolve sugar.

Add juice of oranges and lemon. Stir. Chill. Makes 6 cups (1.35 L).

Pictured on page 89.

VARIETY PUNCH

A golden punch. Good flavor.

Water	2 cups	500 mL
Granulated sugar	1/3 cup	75 mL
Grapefruit juice	2 cups	500 mL
Pineapple juice	1 cup	250 mL
Juice of oranges	2	2
Juice of lemons	2	2

Combine water and sugar together in pitcher. Stir until sugar dissolves.

Add next 4 ingredients. Chill. Pour over ice in glasses. Makes 5 1/2 cups (1.4 L).

BLENDED PUNCH

Deep yellow color. Both grapefruit and orange can be tasted.

Water	2 cups	450 mL
Granulated sugar	1/3 cup	75 mL
Grapefruit juice	2 cups	450 mL
Juice of oranges	4	4
Juice of lemons	2	2

Put water and sugar in pitcher. Stir to dissolve sugar.

Add grapefruit, orange and lemon juice. Chill. Pour over ice cubes. Makes 6 cups (1.35 L).

Pictured on page 35.

LEMONADE

The good old-fashioned kind complete with little bits of pulp. Syrup keeps for ages and also freezes. Tartaric and citric acid can be purchased at a drug store.

Lemons	12	12
Granulated sugar	10 cups	2.25 L
Tartaric acid	5 tsp.	25 mL
Citric acid	5 tsp.	25 mL
Boiling water	7 cups	1.5 L

Squeeze juice from lemons and put into saucepan over medium heat. Add sugar, tartaric acid, citric acid and water. Stir to dissolve sugar. Remove from heat. Chill. To serve, mix about 1 part lemon syrup to 3 parts cold water. May be mixed in drinking glass for a single serving. Flavor may be strengthened simply by adding more syrup. Makes 16 cups (3.6 L). Strain if desired.

Pictured on cover.

PINK LEMONADE: Add a bit of grenadine for color.

GARLIC BREAD

This loaf is cut right through. Leave bottom of slices attached if you prefer. Good with any kind of meal.

Loaf of French bread, sliced at least 1 inch (2.5 cm) thick	1	1
Butter or margarine, softened	1/2 cup	125 mL
Garlic salt	1/2 tsp.	2 mL
Parsley flakes	1 tsp.	5 mL

Bread may be sliced straight across or on the diagonal. Cut however you prefer.

Mix butter, garlic salt and parsley together well. Spread on both sides of slices. Reshape on long piece of foil. Wrap. Heat on medium grill 10 to 15 minutes. Turn often.

Tare Pointer

Most of us would like an occupation that wouldn't keep us occupied.

CORN MUFFINS

These are a welcome change from bread or dinner rolls for any barbecue meal.

All-purpose flour	1¼ cups	300 mL
Cornmeal	¾ cup	175 mL
Granulated sugar	¼ cup	50 mL
Baking powder	2 tsp.	10 mL
Salt	½ tsp.	2 mL
Egg	1	1
Cooking oil	¼ cup	50 mL
Plain yogurt	1 cup	250 mL

Measure first 5 ingredients into mixing bowl. Stir.

In small bowl beat egg lightly with spoon. Add cooking oil and yogurt. Mix. Add to dry ingredients. Stir just enough to moisten. Fill greased muffin pans ¾ full. Cook by indirect method (see page 149) in closed hot barbecue until an inserted wooden pick comes out clean, about 20 to 25 minutes. Rotate pan at half time. Let muffins cool in pan 5 minutes before removing. These may also be baked in 400°F (200°C) oven for about 20 to 25 minutes. Makes 12 medium muffins. If made ahead wrap in foil and heat on barbecue.

DOTTED MUFFINS: Add 3 tbsp. (50 mL) chopped green onion and 2 tbsp. (30 mL) each of chopped green and red pepper.

Pictured on page 17.

PIZZA ON THE GRILL

A very different treat. Add whatever meat you like.

Tea biscuit mix	2 cups	500 mL
Milk	½ cup	125 mL
Spaghetti or pizza sauce	1 cup	250 mL
Grated mozzarella cheese	2 cups	500 mL
Sliced fresh mushrooms	1 cup	250 mL
Sliced cooked meat, pepperoni, salami, wieners or luncheon meat, fresh or canned	1 cup	250 mL
Chopped green onions	½ cup	125 mL
Red pepper, chopped	½ cup	125 mL
Grated mozzarella cheese	1 cup	250 mL

(continued on next page)

Combine biscuit mix with milk in bowl. Mix to form a soft ball. Press onto greased 12 inch (30 cm) pizza pan. Bake in closed, hot barbecue with lid down over indirect heat, (see page 149) for about 15 minutes. Rotate pan at half-time. Crust should be only partially cooked.

Spread spaghetti sauce over crust.

Layer next 5 ingredients in order given.

Sprinkle with remaining mozzarella cheese. Return to barbecue. Cook the same way as for the crust until piping hot and cheese has melted, about 15 minutes. Cuts into 6 wedges.

Variation: For a special day such as a birthday, add strips of red or green pepper to make the birthday years. It is easy to shape a number.

Pictured on page 35.

BLUEBERRY MUFFINS

Baked outdoors for breakfast or a snack. Excellent with a hint of lemon.

Butter or margarine, softened	$^1/_4$ **cup**	**50 mL**
Granulated sugar	$^1/_4$ **cup**	**50 mL**
Egg	**1**	**1**
All-purpose flour	**1$^3/_4$ cups**	**450 mL**
Baking powder	**4 tsp.**	**20 mL**
Salt	$^1/_2$ **tsp.**	**2 mL**
Grated lemon rind	**1 tsp.**	**5 mL**
Milk	**1 cup**	**250 mL**
All - purpose flour	$^1/_4$ **cup**	**50 mL**
Blueberries, fresh or frozen	**1 cup**	**250 mL**

Cream butter and sugar together well. Beat in egg.

In another bowl combine first amount of flour, baking powder, salt and lemon rind. Stir.

Add flour mixture in 3 parts to batter alternately with milk in 2 parts, beginning and ending with flour mixture.

Stir remaining flour with blueberries to coat berries. Gently stir into batter. Fill greased muffin cups $^3/_4$ full. Bake by indirect heat (see page 149) in closed hot barbecue for about 25 minutes. Rotate pan at halftime. These may be baked in 400°F (200°C) oven for about 25 minutes. Makes 12 medium muffins.

Pictured on page 71.

BARBECUED BISCUIT

Hot biscuits add to any meal whether breakfast, lunch or dinner.

All-purpose flour	2 cups	450 mL
Baking powder	4 tsp.	20 mL
Baking soda	$1/2$ tsp.	2 mL
Salt	$3/4$ tsp.	4 mL
Butter or margarine	3 tbsp.	50 mL
Sour milk, see Note	$3/4$ cup	175 mL

Measure flour, baking powder, baking soda and salt into bowl. Cut in butter until crumbly.

Add sour milk. Mix to form ball. Knead on lightly floured surface 8 to 10 times. Flatten dough to $3/4$ inch (2 cm) height. Place on double thickness of greased foil. Cook over indirect heat (see page 149) in closed hot barbecue. Cook for about 12 minutes. Rotate pan at half-time. Cut into square biscuits or break off pieces. Makes 16.

Note: To make sour milk, add milk to 1 tbsp. (15 mL) vinegar in measuring cup. Stir.

Pictured on page 17.

MAYONNAISE BISCUITS

Cooked on the barbecue or in the oven these are delicious.

All-purpose flour	2 cups	500 mL
Baking powder	2 tsp.	10 mL
Salt	$1/4$ tsp.	1 mL
Milk	1 cup	250 mL
Mayonnaise	$1/2$ cup	125 mL

Stir flour, baking powder and salt together in bowl.

Add milk and mayonnaise. Mix together. Drop onto greased baking pan. Cook on indirect heat (see page 149) in closed hot barbecue for about 20 minutes. Rotate pan at half time. May also be baked in 400°F (200°C) oven for about 20 minutes. Makes 12 biscuits.

Pictured on page 17.

YORKSHIRE PUDDING

This makes a barbecued roast beef meal complete. While beef is resting before slicing, cook this on the barbecue.

All - purpose flour	1 cup	250 mL
Eggs	2	2
Salt	$1/2$ tsp.	2 mL
Milk	1 cup	250 mL
Drippings or cooking oil	2 tbsp.	30 mL

In small mixing bowl beat flour, eggs, salt and milk together well.

Cover bottom of 9 x 9 inch (22 x 22 cm) shallow pan with drippings or cooking oil. Place over hot grill until hot. Pour batter in pan so it is $1/4$ inch (60 mm) thick. Cook on indirect heat (see page 149) in closed hot barbecue for about 30 minutes. Check often. Rotate pan at half time. May also be baked in 450°F (230°C) oven for about 30 minutes. Makes 9 servings.

SOUR MILK QUICKBREAD

No yeast in this. A good flavored loaf. Excellent toasted.

All - purpose flour	4 cups	1 L
Cream of tartar	2 tsp.	10 mL
Baking soda	1 tsp.	5 mL
Granulated sugar	1 tsp.	5 mL
Salt	$1/2$ tsp.	2 mL
Egg, beaten	1	1
Cooking oil	2 tbsp.	30 mL
Sour milk, see Note	$1^1/2$ cups	400 mL

Measure flour, cream of tartar, baking soda, sugar and salt into mixing bowl. Stir.

Add egg, cooking oil and sour milk. Stir to mix well. Dough will be sticky. Turn into greased loaf pan 9 x 5 x 3 inch (23 x 12 x 7 cm). Bake on indirect medium heat (see page 149) for about 45 to 55 minutes. Close lid. This may also be baked in 350°F (180°C) oven for about 45 to 55 minutes. Rotate pan at half-time. Makes 1 loaf.

Note: To make sour milk add milk to $1^1/2$ tbsp. (25 mL) vinegar in measuring cup. Stir.

Pictured on page 143.

BRAN MUFFINS

It's great to cook these outdoors.

Molasses	¹/₄ cup	50 mL
Egg	1	1
Butter or margarine, softened	¹/₄ cup	50 mL
Granulated sugar	¹/₄ cup	50 mL
Milk	³/₄ cup	200 mL
Vanilla	1 tsp.	5 mL
All-purpose flour	1 cup	250 mL
Natural bran or all bran cereal	1 cup	250 mL
Baking powder	2¹/₂ tsp.	12 mL
Salt	¹/₂ tsp.	2 mL

Put first 4 ingredients into mixing bowl. Beat until smooth.

Add milk gradually. Add vanilla.

Measure remaining ingredients into another bowl. Stir well. Add to batter. Stir together until moistened. Fill greased muffin cups ³/₄ full. Cook by indirect heat (see page 149) in closed hot barbecue for about 20 minutes or until an inserted wooden pick comes out clean. Rotate pan at half time. These may also be baked in 400ºF (200ºC) oven for about 20 minutes. Makes 12 medium muffins.

Pictured on page 71.

SEED TOAST

Different and tasty.

Butter or margarine, softened	1 cup	250 mL
Poppy seeds	6 tbsp.	100 mL
Loaf of French bread, thickly sliced	1	1

Combine butter with poppy seeds.

Use about ¹/₂ butter mixture to butter both sides of bread slices. Toast both sides directly on grill over medium-low heat. Spread 1 side of each slice again and serve.

It is easy to joke with a fish. They fall for it hook, line and sinker.

CHICKEN SANDWICHES

You will need a pie iron to make these. Pie irons can be found with camping supplies in a store.

Cooked chicken, flaked or finely chopped	1 cup	250 mL
Ground almonds	1/3 cup	75 mL
Finely chopped celery	1/4 cup	50 mL
Lemon juice	1 tsp.	5 mL
Salt	1/2 tsp.	2 mL
Pepper	1/16 tsp.	0.5 mL
Salad dressing (such as Miracle Whip)	3 tbsp.	50 mL
Bread slices, buttered	12	12

Combine first 7 ingredients together in medium size bowl. Add more salad dressing if desired to make a good spreading consistency.

Put buttered sides of 2 bread slices against inside of pie iron. Place 1/6 filling in center. Close iron. Pull off bread that is around edges. Cook on medium-hot grill until toasted on both sides. Makes 6 sandwiches.

Note: These may be placed in flat wire basket (buttered side out) and cooked over low heat until toasted and hot.

DEVILLED CHICKEN SANDWICHES

Truly an outdoor picnic when a pie iron is used to make these.

Cooked chicken, finely chopped	1/2 cup	125 mL
Hard-boiled eggs, finely chopped	2	2
Green pepper, minced	3 tbsp.	50 mL
Mayonnaise	3 tbsp.	50 mL
Prepared mustard	1 tsp.	5 mL
Salt	1/2 tsp.	2 mL
Pepper	1/8 tsp.	0.5 mL
Bread slices, buttered	8	8

Mix first 7 ingredients together in bowl.

Put buttered sides of 2 slices of bread against inside of pie iron. Place 1/4 filling in center. Close iron. Pull off bread from edges. Cook over medium-hot grill until toasted on both sides. Take a peek once in a while to check. Makes 4 sandwiches.

Note: If desired put sandwiches (buttered side out) in flat wire basket. Cook over low heat until toasted and hot. Pie irons are available where campers' supplies are sold.

TUNA BURGERS

This makes a quick and easy lunch.

Tuna, drained and flaked	6¹/₂ oz.	184 g
Grated medium Cheddar cheese	1 cup	250 mL
Mayonnaise	3 tbsp.	50 mL
Sweet pickle relish	2 tbsp.	30 mL
Chopped green onion	2 tbsp.	30 mL
Prepared mustard	2 tsp.	10 mL
Onion powder	1 tsp.	5 mL
Hamburger buns, split and buttered	6	6

Combine first 7 ingredients in bowl. Mix well.

Spoon into buns. Wrap each bun separately in foil. Cook on barbecue on medium heat, about 5 minutes per side. Hot dog buns may also be used. Just partially split leaving one long side attached and spoon in filling. Makes 6 tuna burgers.

CHEESE BREAD

A good loaf to have ready wrapped in foil. Heat on grill or even in the oven if short of grill space.

Butter or margarine, softened	¹/₂ cup	125 mL
Grated cheese product (see note)	¹/₂ cup	125 mL
Onion powder	¹/₂ tsp.	2 mL
Salt	¹/₈ tsp.	0.5 mL
Loaf of French bread	1	1

Mix butter, cheese, onion powder and salt together.

Slice bread in thick diagonal slices. Spread both sides of slices with butter mixture. Reshape into loaf. Wrap in double thickness of foil. Wrap half a loaf at a time if too long for the barbecue. Heat on medium grill turning often until piping hot, about 10 minutes.

CHEESE TOAST: Butter both sides of thick bread slices with cheese mixture. Toast both sides on medium grill.

Note: Grated cheese product is a Kraft product. It is a very finely grated Cheddar cheese which resembles the texture of commercial grated Parmesan cheese.

BUTTERMILK PANCAKES

Put the griddle on the barbecue and enjoy an outdoor brunch.

All-purpose flour	2 cups	500 mL
Baking powder	2 tsp.	10 mL
Baking soda	1 tsp.	5 mL
Salt	1 tsp.	5 mL
Buttermilk	2 cups	500 mL
Cooking oil	2 tbsp.	30 mL
Eggs	2	2

Measure flour, baking powder, baking soda and salt into bowl. Stir.

Add buttermilk, cooking oil and eggs. Stir until mixed. Heat griddle over medium-hot grill. To test heat, sprinkle a few drops of water on griddle. If drops just sit there and sizzle, it is not hot enough. If they disappear immediately, it is too hot. If they dance all over the griddle, it is just right. Lightly grease griddle for first batch. No grease should be necessary for subsequent pancakes. When top is full of bubbles, turn to brown other side. Serve hot with butter and syrup, see Brown Sugar Syrup, page 86. Makes about 12 pancakes.

Pictured on page 71.

CORNED BEEFWICHES

Made from the shelf these are quick, easy and very good.

Corned beef, broken up	12 oz.	340 g
Ketchup	1/4 cup	50 mL
Dry onion flakes	1 tbsp.	15 mL
Prepared mustard	2 tsp.	10 mL
Worcestershire sauce	1 tsp.	5 mL
Bread slices, buttered	12	12
Mayonnaise (optional)		

Mix first 5 ingredients together in bowl.

Place 6 slices bread buttered side down on counter. Spread with mayonnaise. Cover with filling. Place remaining 6 bread slices over top with buttered side up. Grill in wire basket over low heat until toasted and hot. Makes 6 servings.

BRAN BREAD

With this heavy solid loaf cut into sixteen slices you are getting two and one half tablespoons (thirty seven millilitres) of bran in each slice.

All-purpose flour	4 cups	900 mL
Natural bran	2 cups	450 mL
Bran flakes cereal	$\frac{1}{2}$ cup	125 mL
Baking powder	$2\frac{1}{2}$ tbsp.	35 mL
Salt	2 tsp.	10 mL
Molasses	3 tbsp.	50 mL
Milk	$1\frac{3}{4}$ cups	400 mL
Cooking oil	1 tbsp.	15 mL

Measure flour, bran, bran flakes, baking powder and salt into large bowl. Stir. Make a well.

Add molasses, milk and cooking oil to well. Mix lightly to form a ball. Knead on floured surface about 10 times. Place in greased 9 × 5 inch (23 × 12 cm) loaf pan. Cover with foil that you have puffed up in center to allow for expansion. Place on grill over indirect medium heat (see page 149). Close lid. Cook for about 45 minutes. Rotate pan at half time. Remove from pan. Place loaf on foil sheet. Bake with lid down for about 15 to 20 minutes more. Makes 1 loaf.

Pictured on page 143.

1. Teriyaki Chicken Burgers page 109
2. Better Burgers page 38
3. Potato Salad page 127
4. Pepper Stir-Fry page 135

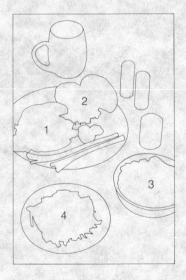

FRESH BREAD

Enjoy freshly baked bread without heating up the kitchen.

Lukewarm water (or milk)	1³/₄ cup	400 mL
Granulated sugar	2 tsp.	10 mL
Salt	1¹/₂ tsp.	7 mL
Butter or margarine	2 tbsp.	30 mL
All-purpose flour	4 cups	900 mL
Instant yeast	1 tbsp.	15 mL

Put lukewarm water into large warmed bowl. A cold bowl will cool down ingredients too much. Add sugar, salt and butter. Stir to dissolve.

Add flour and yeast. Mix well. Knead for 8 to 10 minutes on lightly floured surface. Place in greased 9 x 5 inch (22 x 12 cm) loaf pan. Cover. Let stand in warm, draft-free spot for 1 hour. Brush top with milk. Place on grill over medium heat using indirect heat (see page 149). Close lid. Bake for about 35 minutes. Rotate pan at half-time. Loaf should sound hollow when given a light thump. May also be baked in 375°F (290°C) oven for about 30 to 35 minutes. Makes 1 loaf.

CRAB SANDWICHES

Six round sandwiches cooked in a pie iron from one can of crabmeat. You will find pie irons where camping supplies are sold.

Canned crabmeat, drained, cartilage removed	5 oz.	142 g
Finely chopped celery	¹/₄ cup	50 mL
Chili sauce	2 tbsp.	30 mL
Chopped pimiento	1 tbsp.	15 mL
Hard-boiled egg, chopped	1	1
Bread slices, buttered	12	12

Mix first 5 ingredients together in bowl.

Push 1 slice of bread in each side of pie iron with buttered side against iron. Put ¹/₆ filling in center. Close iron tightly. Tear off bread edges on outside. Cook on a medium-hot grill until toasted on both sides. Makes 6 sandwiches using a round pie iron.

Note: These may be made, put into a flat wire basket and toasted over low heat until hot and browned. Makes only 4 to 5 sandwiches when cooked this way.

Pictured on page 107.

CHOCOLATE DROP CAKE

A quick and easy cake. End results are light, very tender crumb and good.

Sifted cake flour	1 cup	250 mL
Granulated sugar	3/4 cup	175 mL
Baking soda	1 tsp.	5 mL
Baking powder	1/2 tsp.	2 mL
Salt	1/2 tsp.	2 mL
Butter or margarine	1/4 cup	60 mL
Cocoa	1/4 cup	60 mL
Egg	1	1
Sour milk or buttermilk, see Note	1 cup	250 mL
Vanilla	1 tsp.	5 mL

Measure first 5 ingredients into mixing bowl.

Heat and stir butter and cocoa in small saucepan until melted. Pour over dry ingredients.

Break egg into measuring cup. Add sour milk to fill 1 cup (250 mL). Add vanilla. Pour over dry ingredients. Beat all together for 5 minutes. Turn into greased 8 x 8 inch (20 x 20 cm) pan. Lift pan about 5 inches or so (13 cm) from counter and drop. Do this 10 to 12 times. Bake on indirect moderate heat in closed barbecue (see page 149) for about 25 to 30 minutes until an inserted wooden pick comes out clean. Rotate cake at half time. Cake may be baked in 325°F (160°C) oven for 25 to 30 minutes. Serve hot or cold.

Note: To make sour milk, add milk to 1 tbsp. (15 mL) vinegar in measuring cup. Stir.

CHOCOLATE DIP

Great for dipping barbecued fruit, cake, marshmallows, anything.

Semi-sweet chocolate baking squares	8	8
Light cream	2/3 cup	150 mL
Rum flavoring (optional)	1 tsp.	5 mL

Combine all 3 ingredients in small heavy pot. Heat over low heat on grill. Stir often. Makes about 1 1/8 cups (250 mL).

Bite size pieces of fruit grilled and dipped in a delicious sauce makes a fun ending to a cookout.

Orange juice	1$\frac{1}{2}$ cups	350 mL
Lemon juice	1 tbsp.	15 mL
Brown sugar, packed	$\frac{1}{3}$ cup	75 mL
Curry powder	$\frac{1}{2}$ tsp.	2 mL
Cornstarch	1$\frac{1}{2}$ tbsp.	25 mL
Fresh pineapple, cut in chunks	1	1
Oranges, cut in chunks	2 - 3	2 - 3
Maraschino cherries, drained	8	8
Large bananas, peeled, cut in 8 chunks each	2	2
Fresh prune plums, halved, if available	8	8
Whole strawberries	16	16

Whisk first 5 ingredients together in saucepan. Heat and stir over medium heat until it boils and thickens. Cool. Heat on grill when grilling fruit.

Thread fruit on 8 skewers or have guests thread their own. Cook on grill until hot and bananas have browned. Supply forks to dip fruit in sauce. Chocolate Dip, page 56 may be used as well. Makes 8 servings.

Note: Fruit may be brushed with cooking oil if desired when grilling. Refrain from brushing with melted butter as it will end up with a smoky unpalatable flavor.

They don't mind suffering in silence just as long as everybody knows it.

GRILLED APPLES

*Very easy to increase number of apples needed. When these are un-
wrapped you have a great aroma.*

Cooking apples (McIntosh are good), unpeeled, cored	4	4
Brown sugar, packed	1/2 cup	125 mL
Cinnamon	1/8 tsp.	0.5 mL
Raisins or currants	2 tbsp.	30 mL
Butter or margarine	2 tsp.	20 mL

Place each apple on double thickness foil square.

Mix sugar, cinnamon and raisins together. Stuff each hole with mixture.

Put 1/2 tsp. (2 mL) butter over top. Wrap. Place on grill over medium-
hot heat. Cook for about 30 minutes until soft. Turn occasionally.
Serves 4.

BURNT SUGARED FRUIT

Coating fruit in sugar before grilling makes a delicious glazed dessert.

Small baking apples	2	2
Bananas	4	4
Apricots	8	8
Peaches	2	2
Cooking oil	1/4 cup	50 mL
Granulated sugar	1/4 cup	50 mL

Peel apples. Cut into quarters. Core. Cut each quarter in half crosswise
to make 8 chunks per apple. Peel bananas. Cut each into 4 chunks.
If apricots are fresh, cut in half and remove pits. If canned, drain well.
Blot with paper towel to dry. If peaches are fresh, dip in boiling water
1 or 2 minutes until they peel easily. Peel. Cut in half. Remove pits.
Cut each half into 4 chunks making 8 chunks per peach. If using canned
peach halves, drain well. Cut each half into 4 pieces. Blot with paper
towel to dry.

Brush fruit with cooking oil. Coat with sugar. Thread 2 pieces of each
fruit on skewer alternating for looks. Cook over hot grill until sugar has
browned and all fruit is hot. Makes 8 servings.

BANANA CHOCOLATE

Assemble the ingredients and let everyone do their own thing. Great for a birthday party.

Bananas, green tipped

Semisweet chocolate chips
Butterscotch chips
Smooth peanut butter
Honey or corn syrup
Tiny marshmallows

Peel bananas. Place each on double thickness square of foil. Leave whole or slice. Try one or all of the variations listed.

1. Sprinkle banana with chocolate chips.
2. Sprinkle banana with chocolate chips and marshmallows.
3. Sprinkle banana with butterscotch chips.
4. Sprinkle banana with butterscotch chips and marshmallows.
5. Sprinkle banana with chocolate and butterscotch chips.
6. Spread with peanut butter. Slice if desired. Drizzle with honey or corn syrup.
7. Spread with peanut butter. Slice if desired. Sprinkle chocolate chips over top.

Wrap. Place on grill over low heat for about 8 minutes total time. May be turned at half-time.

Those two are just like blisters. They show up when the work is finished.

BLUEBERRY DESSERT

A flavor that's yummy. A color that's intriguing with blueberry yogurt and blueberry fruit. Make ahead and chill.

CRUST

Butter or margarine	¹/₂ cup	125 mL
Graham cracker crumbs	2 cups	500 mL
Granulated sugar	¹/₄ cup	50 mL

FILLING

Unflavored gelatin powder	2 x ¹/₄ oz.	2 x 7 g
Granulated sugar	1 cup	250 mL
Hot water	1 cup	250 mL
Blueberry yogurt	2 cups	500 mL
Sour cream	1 cup	250 mL
Whipping cream (or 1 env. topping)	1 cup	250 mL
Vanilla	1 tsp.	5 mL
Blueberries or saskatoons, fresh or frozen	2 cups	500 mL

Crust: Melt butter in saucepan over medium heat. Stir in graham crumbs and sugar. Measure out ¹/₂ cup (125 mL) for topping. Press the rest into ungreased 9 × 13 inch (22 × 33 cm) pan. Set aside. If you would like crust to be firmer, bake in 350°F (180°C) oven for 10 minutes. Cool.

Filling: Put gelatin and sugar into saucepan. Mix thoroughly. Add water. Heat and stir over medium heat until dissolved. Chill until syrupy.

Fold yogurt and sour cream into gelatin mixture.

Beat cream and vanilla until stiff. Fold in.

Quickly fold in blueberries. If using frozen blueberries, put berries over paper towel in large bottom bowl or pan to thaw. Pat with paper towels before adding. Pour into prepared pan. Sprinkle with reserved crumbs. Chill. Makes 15 servings.

GRILLED PINEAPPLE

Serve these glazed and browned with your next ham barbecue.

Canned pineapple rings, drained	14 oz.	398 mL
Brown sugar, packed	³/₄ cup	175 mL
Water or pineapple juice	4 tsp.	20 mL
Rum or brandy flavoring	1 tsp.	5 mL

(continued on next page)

Lay pineapple slices on hot grill. Use 2 cans if needed. Make some extra sauce to glaze.

Mix brown sugar, water and rum flavoring together. Brush over pineapple. Turn and baste often until browned and glazed. Fresh pineapple rings may also be used. Serve with ham or eat as dessert.

FRUIT KEBABS

Colorful. Perfect choice for letting guests make their own. Small kebabs make good appetizers.

Apricot halves
Cherries, fresh pitted or maraschino
Prune plum halves
Banana chunks
Pineapple chunks
Whole fresh strawberries
Nectarine or peach chunks
Apple chunks
Cantaloupe chunks
Kiwifruit chunks
Orange chunks
Grapefruit chunks
Pitted prunes, plumped

Pound cake, cut in cubes (optional)

Water	1 cup	250 mL
Granulated sugar	1 cup	250 mL
Cornstarch	2 tbsp.	30 mL

Pick 3 to 5 different kinds of fruit being sure to get a variety of color. Put on skewers.

Add cubes of pound cake for an extra treat if desired.

Combine water, sugar and cornstarch in saucepan. Heat and stir over medium heat until it boils and thickens. Brush fruit with this syrup. Cook on greased grill over medium-hot heat. Turn to cook other side. Brush again with syrup. Enough syrup for 6 skewers.

CHOCOLATE DIPPED KEBABS: Make Chocolate Dip, page 56. Use forks to dip fruit and cake. Mmm!

S'MORES

A do-it-yourself treat for all ages. Try the variation as well.

Graham crackers or digestive biscuits
Thin milk chocolate bars or thin
   chocolate mints
Large marshmallows

For each treat you will need 2 graham crackers. Place about 4 squares of chocolate, depending on size, on 1 graham cracker. Place marsh-mallow on fork. Toast over barbecue until soft and melting. Ease it off fork onto chocolate. Cover with second graham cracker. Press down. Chocolate will begin to melt.

Variation: Spread second graham cracker with a thin layer of smooth peanut butter before placing it on top.

CAMPER'S PIE

After trying this dessert with one pie iron you will be buying more so more pies can be made quicker.

White bread slices, buttered	12	12
Pie filling such as cherry, blueberry,	19 oz.	540 mL
raisin, apple, peach		

Push 1 slice of bread in each side of pie iron with buttered side against iron. Put spoonful of pie filling in center. Close iron tightly. Pull off bread around outside edges. Cook on medium-hot grill until toasted on both sides. For 6 servings, there will be pie filling left. Store in refrigerator or freeze or keep making pies until it is used.

Variation: For a sweeter crust sprinkle buttered side of bread with granulated sugar. Tip bread up so excess sugar falls off. Place in pie iron.

Note: Pie irons are carried in stores that carry campers' supplies. There are round ones, square and double ones.

Paré Pointer

The Egyptian girl didn't know what to think when she found out her daddy was a mummy.

BANANAS CARAMEL

Fantastic dessert.

Butter or margarine	1/2 cup	125 mL
Brown sugar, packed	1/2 cup	125 mL
Corn syrup	2 tbsp.	30 mL
Sweetened condensed milk	1/2 cup	125 mL
Green tipped bananas	4	4
Chopped pecans or walnuts	1/3 cup	75 mL

Put first 4 ingredients into heavy saucepan. Heat and stir until boiling. Continue to boil and stir for 5 minutes. Keep stirring as it burns quickly. Remove from heat.

Peel bananas. Place each on double thickness of foil. Cut banana lengthwise or leave whole. Spoon sauce over top. Wrap. Cook on medium grill until hot, about 8 to 10 minutes. Not necessary to turn.

Open packets. Spoon up a bit of sauce over banana. Sprinkle with nuts. Serves 4.

Pictured on cover.

LEMON FREEZE

A snap to make. Let the youngest cook make it.

Whipping cream	1 1/2 cups	375 mL
Milk	1/2 cup	125 mL
Peel of lemon, grated	1	1
Fresh lemon juice	1/3 cup	75 mL
Granulated sugar	1 cup	250 mL
Half shells of lemons	8	8

Measure first 5 ingredients into medium bowl. Stir to dissolve sugar. Place in freezer until frozen, about 2 to 3 hours.

Remove membranes from lemon shells. Cut bottoms from shells so they will stand evenly. Scoop frozen lemon into shells. Makes 8 servings.

Pictured on cover.

GRILLED DESSERT PIZZA

Pure ambrosia. Serve hot with fruit of your choice. Even without fruit it's good.

Biscuit mix	2 cups	500 mL
Milk	1/2 cup	125 mL
Cream cheese, softened	4 oz.	125 g
Cottage cheese	1/2 cup	125 mL
Brown sugar	1/2 cup	125 mL
Egg	1	1
Fresh strawberries		
Fresh raspberries		
Kiwifruit, sliced		
Fresh nectarines, halved and sliced		
Fresh plums, halved and sliced		
Semisweet chocolate chips, melted	1/4 cup	50 mL

Put biscuit mix and milk into bowl. Stir to form a soft ball. Press onto greased 12 inch (15 cm) pizza pan.

Beat cream cheese, cottage cheese and brown sugar in small mixing bowl until smooth. Beat in egg. Spread over biscuit crust. Cook over indirect heat (see page 149) in closed hot barbecue, about 20 minutes. Rotate pan at half-time.

Upon removal from barbecue, add an arrangement of whatever assorted fruit you like.

Drizzle melted chocolate over all. This is good without chocolate too. Cut into 6 to 8 wedges to serve.

Pictured on page 125.

SWEET SHISH KEBABS

You will be surprised how good this is.

Butter or margarine	1/4 cup	50 mL
Brown sugar	1/4 cup	50 mL
Lemon juice	1 tsp.	5 mL
Pound cake, cut in cubes		
Unsliced raisin bread, cut in cubes, or use 2 slices together		
Danish or other sweet pastry, cut in cubes		

(continued on next page)

Put butter, brown sugar and lemon juice into small saucepan. Set on grill to melt. Stir occasionally.

Pierce whatever you are using, or use all three varieties with skewer or long fork. Brush sauce over cubes. Cook over medium-hot grill until toasted, about 5 minutes.

FRUIT AND CAKE KEBABS: Thread skewers with large cubes of pound cake alternated with chunks of oranges. For orange chunks, cut orange in half crosswise then cut each half into 3 chunks. Brush with sauce and grill as above.

Pictured on page 125.

BARBECUED APPLE PIE

With our good produce storage facilities this pie can be made even if it's not apple season. Most everyone's favorite.

Pie crust pastry, your own or a mix

Baking apples (such as McIntosh), peeled and sliced	2 lbs.	900 g
Granulated sugar	1 cup	250 mL
All-purpose flour	2 tbsp.	30 mL
Cinnamon	1/2 tsp.	2 mL
Salt	1/8 tsp.	0.5 mL
Lemon juice	2 tsp.	10 mL

Granulated sugar for topping

Roll pastry and fit into 9 inch (22 cm) pie plate. Trim off excess pastry.

In large bowl mix sliced apples, sugar, flour, cinnamon, salt and lemon juice together well. Pile into prepared crust. Roll out top crust. Dampen outer rim of bottom crust. Cover with top crust. Crimp edges to seal. Cut several slits in top.

Sprinkle with a bit of sugar. Bake on indirect moderate heat in closed barbecue for 45 to 60 minutes until apples are cooked and crust is golden. Rotate pie at halftime. Serves 6.

Pictured on page 107.

WHITE CAKE

Make on day of barbecue meal or just make any day to free your oven up for something else.

Butter or margarine, softened	1/2 cup	125 mL
Granulated sugar	3/4 cup	175 mL
Eggs	2	2
Vanilla	1 tsp.	5 mL
All-purpose flour	2 cups	500 mL
Baking powder	1 1/2 tsp.	7 mL
Salt	1/2 tsp.	2 mL
Milk	3/4 cup	175 mL

Cream butter and sugar together well. Beat in eggs 1 at a time. Add vanilla. Stir.

Mix flour with baking powder and salt. Add in 3 parts alternately with milk in 2 parts beginning and ending with flour mixture. Pour into greased 9 x 9 inch (22 x 22 cm) pan. Place pan on medium grill over indirect heat (see page 149). Close lid. Bake for about 25 to 30 minutes until an inserted pick comes out clean. Rotate pan after 15 minutes. Serve hot with ice cream or cool, and frost. May also be baked in 350ºF (180ºC) oven for about 25 to 30 minutes.

FISH MEAL PACKETS

As the fish cooks, the precooked vegetables heat. A no-fuss meal.

Fish fillets or steaks	1 lb.	454 g
Sliced celery, cooked	1/2 cup	125 mL
Sliced onion, cooked	1/2 cup	125 mL
Tomatoes, peeled and quartered	2	2
Medium potatoes, cooked and sliced	3	3
Salt, sprinkle		
Pepper, sprinkle		
Butter or margarine		
Paprika, sprinkle		

Divide fish into 3 equal amounts. Place each on double thickness foil squares.

Divide vegetables among packets, placing on fish. Sprinkle with salt and pepper. Add dab of butter to each. Sprinkle with paprika. Wrap. Place on grill over medium heat. Close lid. Cook for 10 minutes. Turn. Cook about 5 minutes more. Makes 3 servings.

TROUT IN A BASKET

For the lucky fisherman.

Rainbow trout, pan ready	2 - 6	2 - 6
Lemon juice, drizzle		
Celery salt, sprinkle		
Garlic powder, sprinkle		

Cooking oil

Holding trout open, drizzle cavity with lemon juice followed with celery salt and garlic powder. Place in greased wire basket. Cook over medium-hot grill. Turn and baste with oil often. Allow about 10 minutes cooking time per 1 inch (2.5 cm) thickness of fish. Serve 1 per person providing trout is large enough.

Pictured on page 143.

STUFFED TROUT

Canned crab, drained, cartilage removed	4³/₄ oz.	135 g
Egg	1	1
Dry bread crumbs	¹/₃ cup	75 mL
Sour cream	¹/₃ cup	75 mL
Lemon juice	2 tsp.	10 mL

Mix all 5 ingredients together. Instead of putting lemon juice, celery salt and garlic powder in trout, stuff with mixture. Secure opening with picks. Cook in greased fish basket basting with cooking oil.

TUNA FILLETS

A very easy marinade and a tasty one.

Tuna fillets	1 lb.	454 g
Italian dressing	¹/₂ cup	125 mL

Place tuna in plastic bag. Add Italian dressing. Marinate for 2 hours. Remove fish and place in wire fish rack. Cook on medium grill turning and basting with dressing often allowing about 10 minutes per 1 inch (2.5 cm) thickness. Serves 2 to 3.

CATCH OF THE DAY

Fillets without the skin work equally well when cooked in a wire basket. A very slight tomato flavor. Good.

Fish fillets with skin	1 lb.	454 g
Butter or margarine, melted	1/4 cup	60 mL
Ketchup	3 tbsp.	50 mL
Lemon juice	1 tbsp.	15 mL
Prepared mustard	1/2 tsp.	2 mL
Garlic salt	1/4 tsp.	1 mL

Lay fish in greased wire fish basket.

Mix butter, ketchup, lemon juice, mustard and garlic salt together in small container. Put on side of grill. Brush over fish. Cook on medium-hot greased grill skin side down for about 4 minutes. Turn. Brush with sauce. Cook for about 4 minutes more. Turn and brush with sauce. Cook further if needed for fish to flake when tested with fork. Thin fillets will cook more quickly. Serves 2 to 3.

Note: To get more flavor into fish, marinate in sauce for 20 minutes before grilling. To marinate, use cooking oil instead of butter.

SEEDY MAHI MAHI

A firm fish, mahi mahi holds up well to grilling. Sesame seeds add to the teriyaki flavor.

Soy sauce	2/3 cup	150 mL
Granulated sugar	1 tbsp.	15 mL
Finely chopped ginger	1 tsp.	5 mL
Sherry (or alcohol-free sherry)	2 tbsp.	30 mL
Sesame seeds	1 tbsp.	15 mL
Garlic powder	1/4 tsp.	1 mL
Mahi mahi fillets	2 lbs.	900 g

Combine first 6 ingredients together in bowl. Stir well. Pour into plastic bag.

Add fish. Seal. Marinate 20 minutes. Remove fish and place in greased wire basket on grill over medium-hot heat. Cook about 5 minutes per side. Baste occasionally with sauce. Fish should flake easily when tested with fork. Serves 4 to 5.

SALMON SUPREME

Just right for end chunks of salmon.

Butter or margarine (butter is best)	1/2 cup	125 mL
Juice of lemons	2	2
Barbecue Sauce, see page 84	1/2 cup	125 mL
Finely chopped onion	1/4 cup	50 mL
Brown sugar	1/2 tbsp.	7 mL
Garlic powder, wee pinch		
Section of salmon, cut crosswise with skin intact, opened flat	3 lbs.	1.36 kg

Put butter, lemon juice, barbecue sauce, onion, brown sugar and garlic powder into small saucepan. Stir. Bring to boil. Simmer for 20 to 30 minutes. Sauce may be doubled. Leftover sauce is heated and used for dipping cooked fish.

Brush flesh side of salmon with sauce. Place flesh side down on greased grill over medium heat. Cook until lightly browned, about 15 minutes. Turn so skin side is down. Brush with sauce. Continue to cook without turning until cooked, about 12 minutes. Allow 10 minutes per 1 inch (2.5 cm) of thickness. Fish should flake when tested with a fork. Remove from grill. Peel off burnt skin. Serves 6.

MAHI MAHI

Serve with tartar sauce and lemon juice for a sure fire hit. Juicy and good eating.

Butter or margarine	1/2 cup	125 mL
Lemon juice	4 tsp.	20 mL
Pepper	1/4 tsp.	1 mL
Parsley flakes	1/2 tsp.	2 mL
Mahi mahi	2 1/4 lbs.	1 kg

Combine first 4 ingredients together in small saucepan. Heat on side of grill.

Brush butter mixture over fish. Place fish in greased wire basket. Cook on medium-hot grill, about 5 minutes per side. Allow 10 minutes per inch (2.5 cm) of thickness. Brush with sauce occasionally. Serves 6.

DELUXE SEAFOOD KEBABS

Save for that special occasion.

Lobster tails	2	2
Boiling water		
Scallops	12	12
Shrimp, peeled and deveined	8	8
Red pepper, cut in squares	3	3
Butter or margarine, melted	¼ cup	50 mL

Cook lobster tails in boiling water in covered saucepan until shells turn red. Remove. Cool to handle. Snip either side of shell to remove meat. Slice into a total of 8 pieces.

Thread on skewers (presoak wooden skewers 30 minutes) red pepper, scallop, shrimp, red pepper, lobster, scallop, red pepper, shrimp, scallop, red pepper, lobster, red pepper. Use this as a guide. Change as liked. Add more or less of any one seafood. You may want fewer per skewer for appetizers.

Brush with melted butter. Cook on greased grill over medium-hot heat about 8 to 10 minutes. Turn and baste with butter often. Makes 4 servings.

Pictured on page 125.

1. Barbecued Grapefruit page 13
2. Bran Muffins page 48
3. Blueberry Muffins page 45
4. Breakfast Outdoors page 93
5. Barbecued Oranges page 9
6. Honey Ham Steaks with
   Honey Mustard Sauce page 97
7. Buttermilk Pancakes page 51
   with Brown Sugar Syrup page 86

ORIENTAL SHRIMP KEBABS

A special shrimp feed.

Soy sauce	1/2 cup	125 mL
Sherry (or alcohol-free sherry)	1/2 cup	125 mL
Brown sugar	2 tbsp.	30 mL
Ginger	1 tsp.	5 mL
Garlic powder	1/4 tsp.	1 mL
Shrimp, shelled except for tail, deveined	3 lbs.	1.35 kg

Combine first 5 ingredients in deep bowl. Add shrimp. Let stand for 20 minutes.

Put 6 shrimp on each skewer (presoak wooden skewers 30 minutes). Cook shrimp over medium-hot grill turning and basting often until curled slightly and pinkish in color, about 2 to 3 minutes per side. Serves 6 people about 12 shrimp each. Smaller skewers of 4 shrimp each would make 6 appetizers using 1/3 recipe.

Pictured on page 89.

GRILLED SWORDFISH: Marinate 4 swordfish steaks in sauce rather than shrimp for at least 1 hour up to 4 or 5 hours. Cook on medium grill until it flakes when tested with fork. Turn and brush with sauce often. Total grilling time is about 15 minutes.

SHRIMP AND FISH GRILL

These kebabs are sure to please.

Fish such as salmon, cod or halibut, cut in 1 inch (2.5 cm) cubes	1 3/4 lbs	800 g
Large shrimp, peeled except for tail, deveined	18	18
Large mushrooms, stems removed	12	12
Zucchini slices, 1 1/4 inches (3 cm) thick	12	12
Butter or margarine	1/2 cup	125 mL
Salt	1 tsp.	5 mL
Pepper	1/4 tsp.	1 mL

Arrange first 4 ingredients on 6 skewers (presoak wooden skewers 30 minutes).

Melt butter in small saucepan. Add salt and pepper. Stir. Place skewers on medium-hot grill. Brush with butter. Turn and brush with butter often until fish is browned and cooked, about 6 to 8 minutes. Makes 6 servings.

STUFFED WHOLE SALMON

This salmon is cooked on foil.

Whole salmon, pan ready	4 lbs.	1.8 kg
LEMON STUFFING		
Butter or margarine	6 tbsp.	100 mL
Chopped onion	1 cup	250 mL
Chopped celery	1/2 cup	125 mL
Lemon juice	1/3 cup	75 mL
Dill weed	1/2 tsp.	2 mL
Salt	1/2 tsp.	2 mL
Pepper	1/8 tsp.	0.5 mL
Dry bread crumbs	3 cups	700 mL

Lay salmon on double thickness of greased foil. It doesn't need to be wrapped in foil but can be if you like.

Lemon Stuffing: Melt butter in frying pan. Add onion and celery. Sauté until onion is soft and clear. Remove from heat.

Add lemon juice, dill weed, salt and pepper. Stir.

Add bread crumbs. Mix in. Stuff fish. Put greased foil and fish on medium grill. Grease grill if not using foil. Close lid. Allow 10 minutes per 1 inch (2.5 cm) thickness measured after stuffing at thickest part. Fish should flake easily with fork at thickest part when done. Serves 8.

SALMON 'CHANTED EVENING

Practically no work to this. Easy to double or triple for several more guests. Makes a special evening.

Large thick salmon fillet with skin	4 lbs.	1.8 kg
Salad dressing (such as Miracle Whip)	1/2 cup	125 mL
Ketchup	1/4 cup	60 mL
Brown sugar, packed	1/4 cup	60 mL
Lemon juice	2 tbsp.	30 mL
Parsley flakes (or use fresh)	1 tsp.	5 mL
Salt	1/2 tsp.	2 mL
Pepper	1/8 tsp.	0.5 mL
Worcestershire sauce	1/2 tsp.	2 mL
Parsley for garnish		
Lemon wedges for garnish		

(continued on next page)

Lay salmon skin side down onto double thickness foil that is long enough to cover top loosely. Put on tray for an easy transfer.

In small bowl combine next 8 ingredients. Stir well. Spread over salmon. May be chilled at this point until needed. Lay foil with salmon on medium-hot grill. Now take a skewer and poke holes through salmon right down through foil as well. Do this at 2 inch (5 cm) intervals. Bring foil up over ends of fish but do not do up tight. Leave sides exposed. Close lid. Total cooking time is about 20 minutes. Allow 10 minutes per 1 inch (2.5 cm) thickness plus 5 minutes for foil. To serve cut in 2 inch (5 cm) wide pieces. When you lift pieces skin will remain on the foil. Arrange on warm platter.

Garnish with parsley and lemon. May also be served direct from barbecue to plate. Serves 8.

HALIBUT STEAKS

Very light tomato in the marinade. Cook on the grill or in a basket.

Large halibut steaks (or haddock or salmon), 1 inch (2.5 cm) thick	2	2
CHILI MARINADE		
Vinegar	¹/₂ cup	125 mL
Chili sauce	2 tbsp.	30 mL
Cooking oil	2 tbsp.	30 mL
Brown sugar	2 tbsp.	30 mL
Worcestershire sauce	1 tsp.	5 mL
Onion powder	¹/₄ tsp.	1 mL
Garlic powder	¹/₄ tsp.	1 mL
Chili powder	¹/₄ tsp.	1 mL

Thaw fish if frozen.

Chili Marinade: In shallow pan mix together remaining ingredients. Add steaks. Marinate for about 20 minutes turning occasionally. Place steaks in greased wire basket. Cook over medium-hot grill for about 5 to 6 minutes per side. Baste often with sauce. When done, fish should flake easily when tested with fork. If steak is at least 1 inch (2.5 cm) thick it may be cooked directly on greased grill. Serves 4.

Even when he burns the candle at both ends he isn't bright.

ORANGE SAUCED FISH

This delicate fish from South Pacific waters is now available in many fish markets.

Orange roughy fillets	2 lbs.	900 g
Orange juice	³/₄ cup	175 mL
Grated orange rind	1 tsp.	5 mL
Cooking oil	3 tbsp.	50 mL
White wine (or alcohol-free wine)	3 tbsp.	50 mL
Seasoned salt	¹/₂ tsp.	2 mL
Pepper	¹/₈ tsp.	0.5 mL

Thaw fish completely if frozen.

Mix remaining 6 ingredients together in deep bowl. Add fish. Marinate for 20 minutes. Place fish in greased wire fish basket. Cook over medium-hot heat until fish flakes easily when tested with fork. Serves 5 to 6.

Note: Other delicate fish may be used in this recipe such as cod, sole, flounder, red snapper, plaice, pickerel or perch.

Note: If you don't have a wire basket, place fillets on a sheet of greased foil to avoid breakage. Thin fillets can be cooked without turning.

SHARK!

Eat it. Don't feed it.

Shark fillets	2 lbs.	900 g
Milk to cover		
Soy sauce	¹/₂ cup	125 mL
Orange juice	¹/₂ cup	125 mL
Grated orange rind	1 tsp.	5 mL
Cooking oil	2 tbsp.	30 mL
Chopped fresh parsley	2 tbsp.	30 mL
Lemon juice	2 tbsp.	30 mL
Garlic powder (or 2 cloves, minced)	¹/₂ tsp.	2 mL
Pepper	¹/₂ tsp.	2 mL

Thaw fish completely if frozen. Soak in milk for 1 hour.

Mix remaining ingredients together well in deep bowl. Add fillets. Marinate for 1 hour in refrigerator. Place fillets in greased wire fish basket. Cook over medium-hot grill turning and basting often until tender when pierced with fork, about 7 minutes per side. Makes 4 to 5 servings.

BBQ SHRIMP

These are grilled but they may also be cooked on skewers. Makes a good appetizer.

Large or medium shrimp	1 lb.	454 g
Cooking oil	1/2 cup	125 mL
Small garlic cloves, minced	2	2
White wine (or alcohol-free wine)	1 cup	250 mL
Lemon, sliced	1	1
Chili sauce	1 tbsp.	15 mL
Paprika	1/4 tsp.	1 mL
Salt	1/2 tsp.	2 mL
Pepper	1/8 tsp.	0.5 mL
Cayenne pepper (optional)	1/8 tsp.	0.5 mL

Cut off shrimp heads. Split shell lengthwise to tail. Leaving tail intact remove shell and vein.

Mix remaining 9 ingredients together in deep bowl. Stir well. Add shrimp. Marinate for 1 hour. Cook on medium-hot greased grill brushing with sauce and turning often. Shrimp will curl and turn pinkish when cooked, about 2 to 3 minutes per side. Serves 2.

Pictured on page 89.

TERIYAKI SALMON

A treat you won't soon forget. Try salmon this way for a change. Very good.

Salmon steaks or fillets	4	4
Soy sauce	3/4 cup	175 mL
Brown sugar, packed	1/2 cup	125 mL
Cooking oil	2 tbsp.	30 mL
Ginger	1/2 tsp.	2 mL
Garlic powder	1/4 tsp.	1 mL

Thaw fish if frozen.

Mix soy sauce, brown sugar, cooking oil, ginger and garlic powder together well in deep bowl. Add fish. Marinate for 30 minutes in refrigerator. Place in greased wire fish basket. Cook over medium heat for about 10 minutes per 1 inch (2.5 cm) of thickness. Turn and baste with sauce often. Serves 4.

PEPPERED FISH

Baste this fish with yogurt and crushed peppercorns. Good to zip up your fish.

Plain yogurt	1 cup	250 mL
Black peppercorns, crushed	1^1/$_2$ tbsp.	25 mL
Cooking oil	^{1}/$_4$ cup	50 mL
Paprika	^{1}/$_4$ tsp.	1 mL
Any firm fish, cut in 1 inch (2.5 cm) cubes	2 lbs.	900 g

Mix first 4 ingredients together in deep bowl.

Add fish cubes. Stir gently to coat. Let stand for 30 minutes. Thread onto skewers (presoak wooden skewers 30 minutes). Cook on greased grill over medium-hot heat, turning and basting every 2 to 3 minutes for a total time of about 10 minutes. If you prefer to use a more delicate fish, place skewers in between wire racks. Serves 6.

FILLET GRILL

A simple basting sauce goes on this fish.

Servings of cod, perch or bass
  fillets (or use fish steaks), about
  2 lbs. (1 kg)
	6	6

Butter or margarine, melted	^{1}/$_2$ cup	125 mL
Worcestershire sauce	1 tbsp.	15 mL
Seasoned salt	^{1}/$_2$ tsp.	2 mL
Garlic powder	^{1}/$_4$ tsp.	1 mL
Pepper	^{1}/$_8$ tsp.	0.5 mL

If frozen, thaw fish completely.

Mix butter, Worcestershire sauce, seasoned salt, garlic powder and pepper together in small dish. Brush fillets with mixture. Let stand 15 minutes. Place in greased wire grill basket. Cook over medium-hot heat, basting and turning often until fish flakes when tested with a fork, about 10 minutes total time. Serves 6.

Paré Pointer

She's temperamental all right. Fifty percent temper and fifty percent mental.

NEPTUNE KEBABS

Use red peppers and red onions to add color interest to a white fish kebab.

Haddock or halibut fillets (or other firm fish), cut in 2 inch (5 cm) chunks	2 lbs.	900 g
Red onion chunks	24	24
Squares of red pepper (or use cherry tomatoes)	24	24
Cooking oil	¹/₄ cup	50 mL
Lemon juice	1 tbsp.	15 mL

Thread fish, onion and pepper alternately on skewers (presoak wooden skewers 30 minutes).

Combine cooking oil and lemon juice. Cook fish over medium-hot grill brushing often with lemon mixture until fish flakes when tested with fork, about 7 minutes. Onions remain fairly crisp. If you want them softer precook until tender crisp. Makes 5 to 6 kebabs.

MONKFISH KEBABS: This is a firm textured fish. Use instead of haddock.

SWORDFISH KEBABS: Another firm fish. Use instead of haddock.

LOBSTER

Always a pricey treat indoors or out. Easy to do.

Lobster tails, about 6 oz. (168 g) each	6	6
Butter or margarine, melted	¹/₄ cup	50 mL
Lemon wedges		

To prevent tails from curling while barbecuing, crack or snip shell with kitchen shears lengthwise. Then bend shell backwards (shell side towards shell side) to crack it. Place on medium-hot grill, shell side down.

After 10 minutes, brush meat with melted butter. Turn. Cook for 2 to 3 minutes more. Turn. Brush with butter. Shell will have turned red. Serve with more melted butter and a lemon wedge. To tell when meat is cooked, meat will lose it opaque look and become firm. Serves 6.

It is hard to soar like an eagle if you're working with turkeys.

SHRIMP GRILL

A lemon marinade gives these shrimp a nice mild flavor.

Medium shrimp	1 lb.	454 g
LEMON MARINADE		
Cooking oil	1/2 cup	125 mL
Juice of small lemon	1	1
Rind of lemon, sliced	1	1
Garlic powder	1/4 tsp.	1 mL
Salt	1/4 tsp.	1 mL
Thyme	1/2 tsp.	2 mL
Seasoned salt	1/4 tsp.	1 mL
Pepper, light sprinkle		
Hot pepper sauce (optional)	1/8 tsp.	0.5 mL

Remove heads from shrimp. Slit shell lengthwise to tail. Leave tail intact. Remove shell and vein.

Lemon Marinade: Mix all ingredients together in deep bowl. Add shrimp. Marinate for 1 hour. Stir often. Cook on medium grill turning and basting with marinade often until shrimp is pinkish and curled, about 8 to 10 minutes. Serves 2.

Pictured on page 89.

SHRIMP WITH SHELLS: If you want to be different, leave shells on shrimp. Slit down the back to remove vein but leave shell intact. After they have been barbecued you can eat shells along with the shrimp. They are crunchy and chewable.

TARTAR SAUCE

Fish needs this to be complete.

Mayonnaise	1 cup	250 mL
Sweet pickle relish	1 tbsp.	15 mL
Onion flakes, crushed	1 tsp.	5 mL
Parsley flakes	1/2 tsp.	2 mL

Mix all ingredients together. Chill. Serve with fish. Makes 1 cup (250 mL).

BLUE STEAK TOPPING

Give your steak a zippy finish.

Crumbled blue cheese	1/4 cup	50 mL
Cream	2 tbsp.	30 mL
Worcestershire sauce	1/4 tsp.	1 mL

Mix all 3 ingredients together. Spread over steak as you remove it from the grill or simply put a dab on top. Makes about 1/3 cup (75 mL).

PIQUANT SAUCE

A reddish brown sauce, this is spicy and medium-hot. Brush over meat as it finishes cooking.

Tomato paste	5 1/2 oz.	156 mL
Cider vinegar	1/2 cup	125 mL
Brown sugar, packed	1/4 cup	50 mL
Prepared mustard	1/4 cup	50 mL
Worcestershire sauce	2 tbsp.	30 mL
Salt	1 tsp.	5 mL
Pepper	1/2 tsp.	2 mL
Water	1/2 cup	125 mL

Combine all 8 ingredients together in small saucepan. Stir. Bring to boil. Simmer uncovered until it thickens a bit, about 15 minutes. Makes 2 cups (450 mL).

SPICY RED SAUCE

Just stir all ingredients in a jar and there you have it. Sweet and spicy. Really good. A dark rusty brown color.

Ketchup	1/2 cup	125 mL
Brown sugar	2 tbsp.	30 mL
Vinegar	1 tbsp.	15 mL
Prepared mustard	1 tsp.	5 mL
Worcestershire sauce	1 tbsp.	15 mL
Pepper	1/4 tsp.	1 mL

Measure all ingredients into small jar. Stir well. Chill until ready to baste beef, sausage or chicken. Add more Worcestershire sauce if you want it spicier yet. Makes 2/3 cup (150 mL).

CHEESE SAUCE

A quick, easy sauce. Mellow. Adds greatly to fish.

Condensed cream of mushroom soup	10 oz.	284 mL
Grated medium Cheddar cheese	1/2 cup	125 mL
Cream or milk	2 tbsp.	30 mL
Lemon juice		

Mix soup, cheese and cream together in small saucepan. Put on side of grill to heat. Stir often.

When fish is almost cooked, sprinkle it with lemon juice. To serve, spoon sauce over each serving. Makes 1 1/3 cups (300 mL).

HORSERADISH BUTTER

Pop a coin of this onto meat or fish as you serve it. Tangy and good.

Butter or margarine, softened	1/2 cup	125 mL
Horseradish	1 tbsp.	15 mL
Worcestershire sauce	1 tsp.	5 mL

Cream all 3 ingredients together. Chill until almost firm. Shape into log. Roll in waxed paper. Chill until hard. Slice into coins to serve on steaks or fish. Also good served with roast beef.

BUSH FIRE STEAK SAUCE

Although this is a relatively tame fire now, you can make it as hot as you want.

Ketchup	1/3 cup	75 mL
Worcestershire sauce	1 1/2 tsp.	7 mL
Lemon juice	2 tbsp.	30 mL
Dry mustard powder	1 tsp.	5 mL
Paprika	1/2 tsp.	2 mL
Pepper	1/4 tsp.	1 mL
Hot pepper sauce	1/4 - 1/2 tsp.	1 - 2 mL
Butter or margarine	1/2 cup	125 mL

Combine all 8 ingredients together in saucepan. Place on edge of barbecue. Heat and stir to melt butter. Serve with steaks. Makes 1 cup (250 mL).

Pictured on page 17.

MAÎTRE D'HÔTEL BUTTER

Try this well known butter on meat steaks or fish steaks.

Butter or margarine, softened	½ cup	125 mL
Finely chopped parsley (or ¾ tsp., 4 mL, flakes)	1 tbsp.	15 mL
Lemon juice	1 tbsp.	15 mL
Pepper	⅛ tsp.	0.5 mL

Cream butter and parsley in small bowl. Add lemon juice a few drops at a time creaming after each addition. Mix in pepper. Chill until almost firm. Shape into small log. Roll in waxed paper. Keep chilled. When firm, cut in slices to serve on fish or any steaks.

Variation: Add about 2 tsp. (10 mL) chopped chives to butter before rolling into log.

MOCK HOLLANDAISE SAUCE

As good as the real thing. Use on steaks and also asparagus.

Butter or margarine	3 tbsp.	50 mL
All-purpose flour	2 tbsp.	30 mL
Salt	¼ tsp.	1 mL
Hot water	1 cup	250 mL
Lemon juice	2 tbsp.	30 mL
Egg yolks, beaten	2	2

In small saucepan or top of double boiler, melt butter over medium heat. Mix in flour and salt.

Stir in hot water until it boils and thickens.

Add lemon juice. Place over hot (not boiling) water to keep warm until ready to use.

Put beaten egg yolks into serving bowl. Just before serving, stir mixture into eggs. Makes 1 cup (250 mL).

Paré Pointer

He must be the world's smallest sailor. They said he slept on his watch.

EASY BARBECUE SAUCE

Very quick to make this from the contents of the shelf.

Water	1 cup	250 mL
Ketchup	1 cup	250 mL
Envelope dry onion soup	1	1
Worcestershire sauce	1 tbsp.	15 mL
Oregano	1 tsp.	5 mL
Garlic powder	1/4 tsp.	1 mL
Basil	1/4 tsp.	1 mL
Lemon juice	2 tsp.	10 mL

Measure all 8 ingredients into medium saucepan. Stir. Place over medium heat. Stir often until it boils. Let simmer uncovered for about 10 minutes. Stir often. Makes about 1 1/3 cups (325 mL).

BARBECUE SAUCE

Lots of flavor to this.

Butter or margarine	1 tbsp.	15 mL
Very finely chopped onion	1/3 cup	75 mL
Very finely chopped celery	1/3 cup	75 mL
Garlic clove, minced	1	1
Tomato sauce	2 x 7 1/2 oz.	2 x 213 mL
Brown sugar	2 tbsp.	30 mL
Worcestershire sauce	1 tbsp.	15 mL
Red wine vinegar	1/4 cup	50 mL
Mustard powder	1 tbsp.	15 mL
Bay leaf	1	1
Orange juice	1/2 cup	125 mL
Hot pepper sauce	1/4 tsp.	1 mL

Melt butter in frying pan. Add onion, celery, and garlic. Sauté until soft.

Add next 8 ingredients. Stir. Bring to a boil. Simmer 10 minutes. Discard bay leaf. Makes 2 1/2 cups (575 mL).

Pare Pointer

He had his left side cut off. Now he's all right.

TOMATO SAUCE

Serve this hot and spicy sauce over any fish. Excellent choice.

Canned tomatoes, partly drained	**14 oz.**	**398 mL**
Basil	1/4 tsp.	1 mL
Oregano	1/4 tsp.	1 mL
Thyme	1/4 tsp.	1 mL
Garlic powder	1/4 tsp.	1 mL
Pepper	1/8 tsp.	0.5 mL
Hot pepper sauce	1/4 tsp.	1 mL
Grated Parmesan cheese		

Drain about 1/2 cup (125 mL) juice from tomatoes and reserve. Put tomatoes into saucepan.

Add next six ingredients. Bring to a boil. Simmer for 10 to 15 minutes. Keep hot on side of grill until fish is cooked. If too thick, stir in a bit of reserved juice. Spoon over fish as you serve it.

Sprinkle with Parmesan cheese as desired. Makes about 1 cup (250 mL).

CREAMY DILL SAUCE

Ready to spoon over fish fillets.

Butter or margarine	**3 tbsp.**	**50 mL**
All-purpose flour	**3 tbsp.**	**50 mL**
Salt	1/2 tsp.	2 mL
Pepper	1/8 tsp.	0.5 mL
Dill weed	1/4 tsp.	1 mL
Milk	**1 1/2 cups**	**375 mL**

Melt butter in saucepan. Mix in flour, salt, pepper and dill weed.

Stir in milk until it boils and thickens. Keep on side of grill. Spoon over each serving of fish on each person's plate. Makes 1 1/2 cups (375 mL).

She thought a polygon was a dead parrot.

BROWN SUGAR SYRUP

You can easily make your own syrup for pancakes. Good flavor.

Brown sugar, packed	1 cup	250 mL
Granulated sugar	1 cup	250 mL
Water	1 cup	250 mL
Maple flavoring	1 tsp.	5 mL

Measure all 4 ingredients into saucepan. Heat on grill until boiling and sugar is dissolved. Stir often. Move to side of grill. Ladle over pancakes or serve in a pitcher. Makes about 2 cups (500 mL).

Pictured on page 71.

CURRIED MAYONNAISE

This is so good served with fish.

Mayonnaise	1 cup	250 mL
Vinegar	1 tbsp.	15 mL
Brown sugar	1 tbsp.	15 mL
Prepared mustard	1 tsp.	5 mL
Curry powder	1 tsp.	5 mL

Combine all 5 ingredients in jar. Stir well. Chill. Make this the day before it is to be used so flavors mingle. Makes a generous 1 cup (250 mL).

LAMB STEAKS

Tender and flavorful.

Lemon juice	1/3 cup	75 mL
Parsley flakes	1 tsp.	5 mL
Onion powder	1/2 tsp.	2 mL
Pepper	1/8 tsp.	0.5 mL
Cooking oil	1/2 cup	125 mL
Lamb leg steaks, 3/4 inch (2 cm) thick	4	4

Mix first 5 ingredients together in shallow dish. Stir well.

Add lamb steaks. Turn to moisten. Chill all day or overnight. Turn meat occasionally. A plastic bag works well to marinate. By doing it up tightly it holds liquid around meat. Place meat on greased grill over medium-high heat for about 7 minutes per side for medium-well. Serves 4.

These are outstanding. So tender. So good. This is one to try for your very first lamb meal.

MARINADE

Cooking oil	$^1/_2$ cup	125 mL
Lemon juice	$^1/_4$ cup	50 mL
Garlic powder	$^1/_2$ tsp.	2 mL
Ginger	$^3/_4$ tsp.	4 mL
Pepper	$^1/_8$ tsp.	0.5 mL
Paprika	$^1/_2$ tsp.	2 mL
Crushed cardamom seeds	$^1/_2$ tsp.	2 mL
Meat from leg of lamb, cut in 1$^1/_2$ inch (4 cm) cubes	1$^1/_2$ lbs.	700 g
Onion, cut in 8 pieces	1	1
Green pepper, cut in 8 pieces	1	1

Salt, sprinkle

Marinade: Combine first 7 ingredients in small bowl. Stir well.

Add lamb, onion and green pepper. Let stand in refrigerator for 3 $^1/_2$ to 4 hours. Thread lamb onto skewers (presoak wooden skewers 30 minutes) inserting 2 green pepper and 2 onion chunks here and there on each skewer. Cook on medium-high grill. Turn and baste occasionally, about 15 to 20 minutes.

Sprinkle with salt. Serves 4.

Pictured on page 125.

He heard that hard work never killed anybody but he's not taking any chances.

RACK OF LAMB

One of the most popular lamb dishes.

Racks of lamb, 4 ribs each, with chine bone sawed	6	6
Apple juice (or orange)	1/3 cup	75 mL
Lemon juice	1/3 cup	75 mL
Vinegar	1/4 cup	50 mL
Cooking oil	1/4 cup	50 mL
Soy sauce	2 tbsp.	30 mL
Granulated sugar	1 tbsp.	15 mL
Garlic cloves, minced	2	2
Chopped chives	2 tsp.	10 mL
Dried rosemary	2 tsp.	10 mL

Make a few slits in fat of lamb racks.

Combine remaining 9 ingredients in shallow dish. You may have to use 2 dishes to accommodate all racks. Lay racks in sauce. Spoon sauce all over. Turn occasionally. Marinate for several hours. Remove from marinade. Wrap each rack in a double thickness square of foil. Cook on medium-hot grill for about 20 minutes on meaty side and 10 minutes on bone side. Remove foil. Cook about 15 to 20 minutes more, directly on grill. Turn and baste with marinade often. Serves 6.

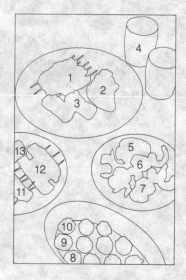

Serve with fresh mint.

Lamb chops, 1 inch (2.5 cm) thick	12	12
Lemon juice	2 tsp.	10 mL
Red wine vinegar	4 tsp.	20 mL
Onion powder	1/4 tsp.	1 mL
Rosemary	1/2 tsp.	2 mL
Cooking oil	2 tbsp.	30 mL
Prepared mustard	1 tsp.	5 mL

Remove excess fat from lamb chops.

Combine remaining ingredients in small bowl. Brush lamb chops. Let stand 15 minutes. Cook over medium-hot grill for about 7 minutes per side for medium. Baste often. Makes 6 servings.

GRILLED SAUSAGE

Always easy and quick. These may be cut into small pieces and served as an appetizer.

Pork sausages	1 lb.	454 g
Water to cover		

Barbecue Sauce, see page 84 (or use ketchup)

Prick each sausage in 3 or 4 places so fat can escape. Boil sausages in water for about 5 minutes. Drain. Place on grill over medium heat.

Baste with barbecue sauce often as you turn sausages. Cook until well glazed and no pink remains. Serves 3 to 4.

WIENER GRILL: Omit boiling. Brush with barbecue sauce as wieners are heated.

GARLIC GRILL: Whole ring of sausage may be grilled then sliced in thin pieces for an appetizer or in thick or long pieces for a main course. Very good when hot.

BRATWURST: You will need about 2 bratwurst per person. Prick sausage several times to allow fat to escape. It is best to boil them in water for 5 minutes. Grill over medium heat for about 8 to 10 minutes per side. A popular choice.

KNACKWURST: Another popular choice. Cook the same as Bratwurst allowing perhaps a bit less cooking time.

FRANKFURTERS DELUXE

Cheese and bacon. Now that's a good dog.

Wieners	6	6
Process Cheddar cheese slices, cut in narrow strips	4 - 6	4 - 6
Bacon slices	6	6
Hot dog buns, split, toasted and buttered	6	6

Slice wieners lengthwise. Insert a cheese strip between halves. Put back together and wrap with a strip of bacon diagonal style. Insert wooden picks to hold. Soak wooden picks in water for 20 minutes first. Cook on medium-hot grill turning once until bacon is done.

Insert in toasted bun. Makes 6 servings.

FRANKS AND BEANS

A whole mess of stuff in foil that ends up in a bun. Beans, cheese and wieners.

Wieners	8	8
Prepared mustard		
Canned baked beans, drained	8 oz.	227 mL
Hot dog buns, split, toasted and buttered	8	8
Sweet pickle relish	¹/₄ cup	50 mL
Process cheese spread		

Slice wieners in half lengthwise not quite through meat. Spread cut surfaces with mustard. Lay each wiener on double thickness of foil. Insert about 2 tbsp. (30 mL) of beans in each wiener. Wrap. Cook on medium-hot grill turning once until hot, about 5 minutes.

Spread buns with relish on bottom and cheese on top. Unwrap wieners and beans and serve in buns. Makes 8 servings.

Pictured on page 35.

Pare Pointer

If a priest and a cobbler came to visit would you have heavenly soles?

Sausages and peaches are served under a biscuit topping with syrup poured over all. Baked in one pan.

Small pork sausages	1 lb.	454 g
Water to cover		
Canned sliced peaches, drained, juice reserved, cut in half	14 oz.	398 mL
Tea biscuit mix	2 cups	450 mL
Milk	3/4 cup	175 mL
Egg	1	1
PEACH SYRUP		
Reserved juice		
Brown sugar, packed	1 cup	250 mL
Water	1/2 cup	125 mL
Maple flavoring	1/2 tsp.	2 mL
Cornstarch	2 tbsp.	30 mL

Prick sausages with fork. Boil in water for 5 minutes. Drain. Grill sausage over medium heat until no pink remains. Cut into bite size pieces. Place in greased 9 x 9 inch (22 x 22 cm) pan.

Scatter peach slices evenly among sausage pieces.

Mix biscuit mix, milk and egg together. Pour over sausage-fruit layer. Bake over indirect heat (see page 149) at medium temperature in closed barbecue. This may also be baked in 350°F (180°C) oven. Bake about 30 minutes until an inserted wooden pick comes out clean. Rotate pan at half-time.

Peach Syrup: Combine all 5 ingredients in small saucepan. Heat and stir over medium heat until it boils and thickens. Spoon over above servings. Makes 6 servings.

Pictured on page 71.

Santa's reindeers go on roof tops. That makes them deer devils.

FRANKLY KRAUT

Wieners and sauerkraut are a natural.

Wieners	12	12
Prepared mustard		
Sauerkraut, drained	14 oz.	398 mL
Hot dog buns, split, toasted and buttered	12	12
Ketchup		
Chopped onion, raw or cooked	1 cup	250 mL

Slice wieners in half lengthwise not quite through meat. Spread cut surfaces with mustard. Place each wiener on double thickness of foil. Fill with about 2 tbsp. (30 mL) sauerkraut. Wrap. Cook on medium-hot grill, turning once until hot, about 5 minutes.

Spread top inside of bun with ketchup and bottom inside of bun with onion. Unwrap wieners and insert in buns. Serves 6 people, 2 each.

Pictured on page 35.

SPARERIBS

Crusty on the outside and moist on the inside.

Pork spareribs	4 lbs.	1.8 kg
Soy sauce	$\frac{1}{4}$ cup	50 mL
Sherry (or red wine vinegar)	2 tbsp.	30 mL
Oyster sauce	1 tbsp.	15 mL
Brown sugar, packed	$\frac{1}{4}$ cup	50 mL
Ginger	$\frac{1}{4}$ tsp.	1 mL
Garlic powder	$\frac{1}{4}$ tsp.	1 mL

Cut spareribs into sections for easy turning.

Mix remaining ingredients together in small bowl. Brush over ribs on tray. Chill. Let stand for 3 to 4 hours. Place ribs on grill over low heat. Cook, turning often until tender, about 50 minutes. Ribs must be basted often while cooking so as not to dry. Cut into serving size pieces. Serves 4 to 6.

If you have a cob of corn and a pain you would have an earache.

Once cooked, this boneless loin can be cut and served in no time. Succulent.

Pork loin, boned and rolled	4¹/₂ **lbs.**	**2 kg**
MEAT SAUCE		
Chili sauce	¹/₃ **cup**	**75 mL**
Water	¹/₃ **cup**	**75 mL**
Cider vinegar	**3 tbsp.**	**50 mL**
Cooking oil	**2 tbsp.**	**30 mL**
Worcestershire sauce	**1 tbsp.**	**15 mL**
Brown sugar	**1 tbsp.**	**15 mL**
Prepared mustard	**2 tsp.**	**10 mL**
Paprika	**1 tsp.**	**5 mL**
Onion powder	**1 tsp.**	**5 mL**
Pepper	¹/₄ **tsp.**	**1 mL**

Secure meat on spit. Remove grill. Place drip pan directly beneath meat over lava rock. Add 2 inches (5 cm) water to pan. Cook in covered barbecue over low heat for about 1¹/₂ hours. If cooking over charcoal spread coals apart to make room for drip pan below meat and on floor of barbecue.

Meat Sauce: Mix all 10 ingredients together. Brush over meat several times while it finishes cooking. Test with meat thermometer. Serves 8.

Note: Meat Sauce is excellent for chicken as well as pork chops.

OTHER COOKING METHODS
Roast may be placed on roast rack or directly on grill over drip pan without water and cooked by indirect heat, see page 149.

Roast may be placed on roasting rack on grill over drip pan with water. Use low heat in closed barbecue.

Roast may be cooked in covered roaster (or uncovered) set right on grill over low heat. No drip pan required. Close cover of barbecue.

SPIT COOKING: Boneless meat is much easier to balance on the spit. Place drip pan with water in it beneath meat unless using charcoal in which case put drip pan on floor of barbecue surrounded by charcoal. No need to use water in drip pan. Cook at moderate temperature. (With lid closed, use low flame. With open barbecue, use medium-high flame.) Meat is self basting. Juices should be bubbling on the surface when checked. Use a meat thermometer to check doneness. Do not let drip pan with water run dry.

RAJUN CAJUN RIBS

More heat can be added to suit your taste. Just add more cayenne pepper.

Pork spareribs	3 lbs.	1.4 kg
Boiling water to cover		
RAJUN CAJUN SAUCE		
Ketchup	$2/3$ cup	150 mL
Cayenne pepper (or more to taste)	$1/4$ tsp.	1 mL
Pepper	$1/8$ tsp.	0.5 mL
Garlic powder	$1/8$ tsp.	0.5 mL
Chili powder	$1/8$ tsp.	0.5 mL

Cut ribs into easy to handle portions. Cook in boiling water until tender, about 1 hour. Drain. Cool.

Rajun Cajun Sauce: Combine all 5 ingredients together in small bowl. Brush over ribs. Place ribs on grill over medium-hot heat. Turn and baste often, about 10 minutes until well glazed and hot. Serves 4.

Pictured on cover.

PINEAPPLE HAM STEAK

The cloves in the basting sauce add a different and good flavor to this ham.

Ham steaks, $3/4$ inch (2 cm) thick	2	2
Brown sugar, packed	$1/4$ cup	50 mL
Cornstarch	1 tbsp.	15 mL
Paprika	1 tsp.	5 mL
Cloves	$1/4$ tsp.	0.5 mL
Pineapple juice	1 cup	250 mL

Slash fat on steaks at intervals to prevent curling. Remove excess fat. Ham may be cut for easier handling and serving or left whole.

Put brown sugar, cornstarch, paprika and cloves in small saucepan. Mix well.

Stir in pineapple juice. Heat and stir until it boils and thickens. Lay ham on greased grill over medium-high heat to brown both sides slightly. Brush with sauce turning and brushing often, just until hot and glazed. Serves 6.

HONEY HAM STEAKS

A foolproof meat. Needs only to be browned a bit. Sauce gives a nicer browning without ham drying out.

Ham steaks	4 lbs.	1.75 kg
HONEY MUSTARD SAUCE		
Brown sugar, packed	1/2 cup	125 mL
Honey	2 tbsp.	30 mL
Butter or margarine	1/2 cup	125 mL
Soy sauce	2 tsp.	10 mL
Prepared mustard	2 tsp.	10 mL

Remove excess fat from steaks. Leave whole or cut for easy handling.

Honey Mustard Sauce: Combine all ingredients in small saucepan. Heat and stir until melted and blended. Brush over ham to barbecue or fry. Makes about 3/4 cup (200 mL).

Place steaks on grill over medium-high heat. Brush tops with Honey Mustard Sauce. When lightly browned, turn and brush other side with sauce. Leave over grill only to glaze and heat through so as not to dry meat. Being already cooked, it doesn't take long. Serves 8 generously.

Pictured on page 71.

PEANUT BUTTER FRANKS

You will be surprised how good this is.

Wieners	6	6
Smooth peanut butter		
Bacon slices	6	6
Hot dog buns, split, toasted and buttered	6	6

Slice wieners lengthwise. Spread cut sides with peanut butter. Put back together. Wrap bacon around in diagonal style securing with wooden picks (presoak wooden picks 20 minutes). Cook on medium-hot grill, turning once until bacon is cooked.

Insert in toasted bun. Makes 6 servings.

Pictured on page 35.

CREOLE CHOPS

A tomato-flavored sauce makes these chops out of the ordinary.

Pork chops, ³/₄ inch (2 cm) thick	6	6
Tomato paste	5¹/₂ oz.	156 mL
Water	¹/₃ cup	75 mL
Brown sugar, packed	¹/₄ cup	50 mL
Vinegar	1¹/₂ tbsp.	25 mL
Worcestershire sauce	1 tsp.	5 mL
Onion powder	¹/₄ tsp.	1 mL
Chili powder	¹/₄ tsp.	1 mL

Remove excess fat from chops to reduce flare-up.

Mix remaining 7 ingredients together in small bowl. Pour into plastic bag. Add chops. Seal bag. Let marinate for at least 1 hour. Place chops on grill over medium heat. Cook for a total of about 15 minutes. Turn and brush with sauce occasionally. Makes 6 servings.

QUICK SOY CHOPS: Baste pork chops often with soy sauce as they cook. These are so simple and are very good.

BARBECUE CHOPS: Baste with your favorite barbecue sauce, see page 84. Good.

LEMON DILL CHOPS

Complete these chops with Lemony Dill Sauce. Excellent.

Good size pork chops	8	8
LEMONY DILL SAUCE		
Mayonnaise	6 tbsp.	100 mL
Dijon style mustard	¹/₄ cup	60 mL
Lemon juice	¹/₄ cup	60 mL
Dill weed	1 tsp.	5 mL

Remove excess fat from pork chops.

Lemony Dill Sauce: Mix all 4 ingredients together in small bowl. Pour into plastic bag. Add chops. Seal bag. Marinate for at least 30 minutes. Remove meat to grill over medium heat. Cook for about 15 minutes total time. Turn and brush with sauce occasionally. Makes 8 servings.

MAUI PORK CHOPS

After using this pineapple sauce for a marinade it is heated and used as a sauce. It is an exceptionally good sauce.

Pork chops, ³/₄ inch (2 cm) thick	6	6
MAUI SAUCE		
Crushed pineapple with juice	19 oz.	540 mL
Soy sauce	¹/₂ cup	125 mL
Granulated sugar	2 tbsp.	30 mL
Ginger	¹/₂ tsp.	2 mL
Garlic powder	¹/₂ tsp.	2 mL
Pepper	¹/₄ tsp.	1 mL

Trim excess fat from chops.

Maui Sauce: Put all 6 ingredients into bowl. Stir. Add pork chops. Marinate for 2 hours in refrigerator. Place chops on greased grill over medium heat. Turn and baste every 3 to 4 minutes until cooked, about 12 to 15 minutes total time.

Heat marinade in saucepan on side of grill. Simmer for a few minutes. Serve with chops. Makes 6 servings.

APPLE PORK STEAK

These have a mild apple flavor. Serve with apple sauce to complement.

Pork steaks, cut ³/₄ inch (2 cm) thick	8	8
Apple juice	1 cup	250 mL
Soy sauce	¹/₂ cup	125 mL
Granulated sugar	¹/₃ cup	75 mL
Vinegar	1 tbsp.	15 mL
Rum flavoring	2 tsp.	10 mL
Prepared mustard	1 tsp.	5 mL

Remove excess fat from steaks.

Measure remaining 6 ingredients into deep bowl. Add chops. Marinate at least two hours or overnight in refrigerator. Place chops on greased grill over medium heat. Baste with sauce. Continue to baste and turn until done, about 15 minutes total time. Makes 8 servings.

CROWNED DOGS

Hot dogs dressed up. Impressive and very different.

Wieners	2 lbs.	900 g
Envelopes stuffing mix, prepared according to directions on box	2 × 6 oz.	2 × 170 g
Prepared mustard	2 tbsp.	30 mL
Soy sauce	2 tbsp.	30 mL
Brown sugar	2 tbsp.	30 mL

Thread a large needle with string. Do not use thread as it will cut through wieners. Put needle through center of every wiener. Lay joined wieners flat on counter. The length of joined wieners should measure about 14 inches (35 cm) or less if you prefer.

Squeeze some stuffing together in a ball and place on center wieners. Bring ends up together around stuffing. Tie string together. Cut off long ends of string. Stand upright on foil pie plates. Use 2 or 3 plates for strength or use a pizza pan. Add remaining stuffing.

Combine mustard, soy sauce and brown sugar together in small bowl. Brush wieners with sauce. Place pan with wiener roast on medium grill using indirect heat (see page 149). Close lid. Brush wieners with sauce several times while cooking, about 45 minutes until heated through. Rotate pan at half time. Serves 8.

Pictured on page 35.

JAVA RIBS

Different from the usual. Good flavor. Ribs are precooked which means barbecuing time is less.

Pork spareribs	6 lbs.	2.75 kg
Water to cover		
Bay leaves	2	2
Thyme	3/4 tsp.	4 mL
Onion salt	1/2 tsp.	2 mL
Pepper	1/2 tsp.	2 mL
JAVA MARINADE		
Prepared strong coffee	1 1/4 cups	300 mL
Ketchup	1 1/4 cups	300 mL
Brown sugar, packed	2/3 cup	150 mL
Cider vinegar	1/2 cup	125 mL
Worcestershire sauce	4 tsp.	20 mL

(continued on next page)

Cut ribs into easy to handle size pieces, about 3 ribs each. Place in large pot. Add water to cover. Add bay leaves, thyme, onion salt and pepper. Bring to a boil. Boil slowly, covered, for about 1 hour until tender but not so tender that the meat falls away from the bones. Drain. Cool a bit.

Java Marinade: Measure next 5 ingredients into large bowl. Stir to dissolve sugar. Add ribs. Make sure all are coated with marinade. Let stand at room temperature for 30 minutes. Cook on greased grill over medium-hot heat. Brush with marinade and turn often for 10 to 20 minutes until sizzling and glazed. Serves 8 to 10.

Pictured on page 17.

RIBS ON A SPIT

These cook to a glistening finish even without brushing with anything. However, they are also delicious with a sauce.

Rack of pork ribs	3¹/₂ lbs.	1.6 kg
Barbecue Sauce, see page 84 (optional)		

Ribs should be about 4 inches (10 cm) long. A rack that hasn't been sawed in half will have ribs that are too long. Thread ribs on rotisserie rod accordian fashion. Start with narrow end so longer ribs are in the center with shorter ribs on each end. Remove grill. Place drip pan or pans directly under ribs under grill. Pour about 2 inches (5 cm) of water into pans. Rotate over low heat for 1¹/₂ to 2 hours. Add water to drip pans as needed. If using barbecue with charcoal, scrape charcoal away from center. Place drip pans on floor of barbecue. No need to add water. Close lid.

If you plan to baste with Barbecue Sauce, begin to brush ribs with sauce after 30 minutes. Brush every 10 minutes until done. Meat on edges will be crisp but inside should be moist and tender. Meat should pull away from bone cleanly and easily when cooked. Cut between ribs to serve. Serves 4 to 5.

Paré Pointer

Does hypnotism mean rheumatism in the hip?

PORK KEBABS

Pork and apple — always a good combination.

Boneless pork butt, cut 1 inch (2.5 cm) thick	2.2 lbs.	1 kg
Vinegar	3 tbsp.	50 mL
Cooking oil	2 tbsp.	30 mL
Onion flakes, crushed	2 tbsp.	30 mL
Chili powder	1 tbsp.	15 mL
Ginger	1/2 tsp.	2 mL
Seasoned salt	2 tsp.	10 mL
Unpeeled apples, halved crosswise, each half cut in 4 chunks		

Cut meat into strips about 1/2 inch (12 mm) wide. Then cut each strip into squares.

Mix vinegar, cooking oil, onion flakes, chili powder, ginger and seasoned salt together well in deep bowl. Add pork. Stir to coat every piece. Cover. Marinate in refrigerator 2 to 3 hours. Stir occasionally.

Thread pork on skewers (presoak wooden skewers 30 minutes) alternating with apple using a few pieces for an appetizer and more for a main course. Cook over medium grill until no pink remains inside, about 15 to 20 minutes. Turn often as it cooks, basting with sauce each time. Makes 12 appetizers and 6 main course.

Pictured on page 125.

Variation: Add green or red pepper and onion pieces to kebab before grilling.

Maybe oranges don't think but we all know how they concentrate.

BOBBED WIENERS

At last a kebab that the young set likes.

Wieners, cut in 4 pieces crosswise	12	12
Bacon slices, cut in 6 pieces crosswise	8	8
FRANKFURTER SAUCE		
Chili sauce	1/2 cup	125 mL
Brown sugar	2 tbsp.	30 mL
Vinegar	2 tbsp.	30 mL
Worcestershire sauce	1/4 tsp.	1 mL
Onion powder	1/4 tsp.	1 mL

Thread each of 6 skewers (presoak wooden skewers 30 minutes) with 8 pieces of wiener and 8 pieces of bacon.

Frankfurter Sauce: Mix all ingredients together in small bowl. Cook wieners over medium-hot grill basting with sauce and turning often until hot and glazed and bacon is cooked about 10 minutes. Bacon can also be looped up and down to fit in and over each piece of wiener instead of cutting it. You may need more bacon but the looks are worth it. Serves 6.

CHARCOALED HAM STEAK

A sure way to entertain when you begin with meat that is already cooked. So easy.

Ham steaks, 3/4 inch (2 cm) thick	2	2
Condensed orange juice	1/4 cup	50 mL
Brown sugar, packed	1/2 cup	125 mL
Mustard powder	1/2 tsp.	2 mL

Slash edges of ham steaks to prevent curling or cut into serving size pieces. Remove excess fat.

In small bowl mix orange juice, sugar and mustard powder. Put ham on greased grill over medium-high heat. Lightly brown each side. Brush with sauce. Turn often and brush with sauce each turn. Do not overcook. Cook just until it glazes nicely. Serves 6.

SMOKED PORK CHOPS: These chops need only to be heated. Cook as for ham steaks whether plain or basted with Orange Sauce, page 112.

BEST PORK CHOPS

This marinade works best with fat-free chops.

MARINADE

Water	½ cup	125 mL
Soy sauce	⅓ cup	75 mL
Cooking oil	¼ cup	60 mL
Lemon and pepper seasoning	3 tbsp.	50 mL
Garlic cloves, minced	2	2
Pork chops, all fat removed	6	6

Marinade: In deep bowl combine water, soy sauce, cooking oil, lemon pepper and garlic. Stir well.

Place fat-free meat into marinade. Marinate for at least 45 minutes. Cook on greased grill over medium heat for about 25 minutes total time. Turn and baste during cooking time. Makes 6 servings.

CHICKEN ON A SPIT

As chicken rotates it bastes itself. This is good as is but for extra flavor brush with barbecue sauce or marmalade.

Chicken, oven ready	4 lbs.	1.8 kg
Barbecue Sauce, see page 84 (optional)		
Orange marmalade (optional)		

With string, tie wings to body. Affix on spit. Tie legs and tail to spit. Tighten forks. Place drip pan under chicken over lava rock. Add water to pan. Add more water as needed. If cooking over charcoal use indirect heat (see page 149). Cook over low heat with lid closed. Cooking time will be about 1¼ hours. If desired, when chicken is almost done, brush with sauce or marmalade several times during last few minutes. Meat will pull away from bottom part of legs when cooked. Serves 5 to 6.

Paré Pointer

You will find that young people today think a town square is a person.

LEMON GARLIC CHICKEN

Very convenient to have these chilled and waiting to be grilled. Being boneless, they cook quickly. Excellent choice.

Juice of lemon	1	1
Cooking oil	1 tbsp.	15 mL
Garlic clove, minced	1	1
Lemon and pepper seasoning	$1/2$ tsp.	2 mL
Oregano	$1/8$ tsp.	0.5 mL
Cayenne, just a pinch		
Chicken breasts, skin removed, halved and boned	4	4

Put first 6 ingredients into small bowl. Mix well.

Brush over boneless breasts. Let stand at room temperature for 30 minutes or pile into a bowl and leave in refrigerator for a few hours. Cook on greased grill over medium-high heat turning now and then for a total time of about 15 minutes. Serves 4.

TURKEY PATTIES

Use as a main course meat or put into buns to eat as a burger.

Ground turkey or chicken	1 lb.	454 g
Dry bread crumbs	$1/3$ cup	75 mL
Grated carrot	$1/3$ cup	75 mL
Salt	1 tsp.	5 mL
Pepper	$1/4$ tsp.	1 mL
Thyme	$1/2$ tsp.	2 mL
Chicken bouillon powder	1 tsp.	5 mL
Hot water	$1/4$ cup	50 mL
Cooking oil		

Mix first 6 ingredients together in bowl.

Dissolve bouillon powder in hot water. Add to meat mixture. Mix well. Shape into $1/2$ inch (12 mm) thick patties.

Brush with cooking oil. Cook over medium-hot grill until browned. Turn, basting with more cooking oil if it looks dry. Cook until browned and no pink remains in meat, about 8 to 10 minutes per side. Makes about 5 to 6 patties.

SAUCED CHICKEN

Make these chicken halves as hot as you like. Just increase pepper and hot pepper sauce.

Tomato juice	¹/₂ cup	125 mL
Chopped onion	¹/₂ cup	125 mL
Tomato juice	¹/₂ cup	125 mL
Worcestershire sauce	2 tbsp.	30 mL
Cooking oil	¹/₄ cup	50 mL
Pepper	1 tsp.	5 mL
Hot pepper sauce	¹/₄ tsp.	1 mL
Vinegar	³/₄ cup	175 mL
Salt	1¹/₂ tsp.	7 mL
Granulated sugar	1¹/₂ tsp.	7 mL
Chicken halves	8	8

Run first amount of tomato juice and onion through blender. Pour into bowl.

Add next 8 ingredients. Stir. Brush over chicken. Let stand for 30 minutes.

Place chicken cut side down on grill over medium heat. Brush with sauce. Cook turning and brushing with sauce often. Total time about 1 hour. Close lid to hasten cooking. Serves 8.

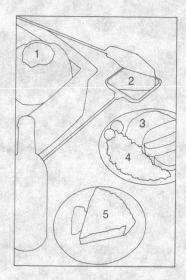

TERIYAKI CHICKEN BURGERS

A grilled chicken breast makes a fine burger.

Soy sauce	1/4 cup	50 mL
Brown sugar	2 tbsp.	30 mL
Ginger	1/4 tsp.	1 mL
Garlic powder	1/4 tsp.	1 mL
Large chicken breasts, halved, skin and bone removed	3	3
Pineapple rings	6	6
Hamburger buns, split and buttered	6	6
Lettuce leaves	6	6
Tomato slices	6	6
Mayonnaise, as desired		

Combine soy sauce, sugar, ginger and garlic powder in small bowl. Stir.

Brush chicken with sauce. Cook on grill over medium heat for about 20 minutes total time. Turn and brush with sauce often.

Brush pineapple rings with sauce. Place on grill when chicken is almost cooked. Brown both sides.

On bottom half of bun put lettuce, tomato, mayonnaise, chicken and pineapple ring. Add top of bun. Makes 6 chicken burgers.

Pictured on page 53.

CHICKEN TERIYAKI: Marinate chicken in sauce for 30 minutes. Cook as above. Serve as main course instead of in buns.

SPECIAL CHICKEN

This chicken has a delicious crust.

Chicken halves or breasts	4	4
Chili sauce	1/2 cup	125 mL
Envelope dry onion soup	1	1
Apricot jam	1/4 cup	50 mL

Cook chicken on greased grill over medium heat for 15 minutes on each side.

Mix next three ingredients together. Brush chicken with sauce. Turn and brush other side with sauce. Baste and turn often until glazed well. Total time, about 1 1/4 hours for chicken halves. Allow less time for breasts. Serves 4.

STUFFED CHICKEN BREASTS

Roll these up ahead of time. Ready to grill. A bit of stuffing is in every roll.

Large boneless chicken breasts, halved, skin intact	3	3
Dry bread crumbs	1 cup	250 mL
Grated carrot	1/4 cup	50 mL
Parsley flakes	1/2 tsp.	2 mL
Celery flakes	1/2 tsp.	2 mL
Onion flakes	1 tsp.	5 mL
Poultry seasoning	1/4 tsp.	1 mL
Chicken bouillon powder	1/2 tsp.	2 mL
Hot water	1/4 cup	50 mL
Butter or margarine, melted	1/4 cup	50 mL

Lay the chicken breasts skin side down. Pound flat.

Measure bread crumbs, carrot, parsley, celery and onion flakes and poultry seasoning into bowl.

Stir bouillon powder into hot water. Add gradually to crumb mixture until moist enough to hold together when squeezed lightly. Place spoonful on each chicken piece. Roll, tucking in ends. Seal with wooden picks that have been soaked in water for 20 minutes or more.

Baste with butter. Cook on greased grill over medium heat turning every 5 minutes. Baste with butter with each turn. You may need to melt a bit more butter to use for basting. Total cooking time, 20 to 30 minutes. Makes 6 servings.

Pictured on cover.

DINNER PACKETS

A meal in one. Contains chicken, potato, carrots and onions.

Small chicken breasts, halved	3	3
Drumsticks	6	6
Medium potatoes, sliced	6	6
Medium carrots, sliced	6	6
Medium-small onions, sliced	6	6
Salt, sprinkle		
Pepper, sprinkle		
Butter or margarine	12 tsp.	60 mL

(continued on next page)

Prepare 6 double thickness foil squares. On each square lay $\frac{1}{2}$ chicken breast, 1 drumstick, 1 sliced potato, 1 sliced carrot, 1 sliced onion. Sprinkle with salt and pepper. Put 2 tsp. (10 mL) butter on each. Wrap to seal. Place on grill to cook. Turn after 20 minutes. Cook about 20 minutes more. Serves 6.

ORANGE DUCK ON A SPIT

If you have never tried tame duck this is the way to go. Good plain or basted with marmalade.

Tame duck	4 lb.	1.8 kg
Orange marmalade	$\frac{1}{2}$ cup	125 mL

Tie wings and neck to body. Put on spit. Tie legs and tail to spit. Put 2 inches (5 cm) of water in drip pan and place on top of lava rock, under grill, directly under duck. Pierce skin here and there to allow fat to escape into drip pan. Add more water to drip pan as needed. If cooking over charcoal use indirect heat (see page 149). Cook for about 1 $\frac{1}{2}$ hours.

When duck is tender, baste with marmalade. Cook for about 10 minutes more. Serve with Orange Sauce. Serves 4.

ORANGE SAUCE

Orange juice	1 cup	250 mL
Grated orange rind	1 tbsp.	15 mL
Lemon juice	1 tsp.	5 mL
Granulated sugar	2 tbsp.	30 mL
Cornstarch	1$\frac{1}{2}$ tbsp.	25 mL
Cider vinegar	1 tbsp.	15 mL

Whisk all ingredients together in small saucepan. Heat and stir until it boils and thickens. Serve on or with duck.

Paré Pointer

The leading cause of dry skin is towels.

CORNISH GAME HENS

These hens are very good just cooked on a spit without any added sauce. Self basting.

Cornish game hens about 1 lb. (454 g) each	**4**	**4**

If frozen, thaw game hens completely. Let thawed hens stand at room temperature for $3/4$ hour. Tie wings to body with string. Put a spit fork on rod. Put rod through body cavity of hens. Tie legs and tail of each hen to rod. Push snugly together. Add second fork to rod. Insert into hens. Tighten.

Remove grill. Place 1 or 2 drip pans directly under hens. Pour 2 inches (5 cm) of water in pans. Place spit on barbecue. Cook over low heat with lid closed. Cook until tender about 45 to 60 minutes. Add water to pans as needed. Serve with Orange Sauce. Allow 1 hen per person.

ORANGE SAUCE

Prepared orange juice	**1 cup**	**250 mL**
Granulated sugar	**$1/4$ cup**	**50 mL**
Lemon juice	**1 tbsp.**	**15 mL**
Grated orange rind	**1 tsp.**	**5 mL**
Cornstarch	**1 tbsp.**	**15 mL**
Water	**1 tbsp.**	**15 mL**

Combine first 4 ingredients in small saucepan over medium heat. Bring to a boil.

Mix cornstarch and water together. Stir into orange juice until it boils and thickens. Divide among plates and set game hen in center or if you like, spoon sauce over hen to serve. Makes enough sauce for 4 hens.

Pictured on page 125.

BBQ CORNISH HENS: As hens are cooking, brush with Teriyaki Marinade, page 27, or Barbecue Sauce, page 84, or marmalade several times towards the last.

QUICK CORNISH HENS: Tie wings to body. Tie legs to tail. Cook in uncovered roaster in 400ºF (200ºC) oven for $3/4$ to 1 hour until tender. At this point you can refrigerate hens and barbecue later, or move directly from roaster to medium-hot greased grill. Brush with barbecue sauce and turn often. Allow 1 hen per person.

BBQ CHICKEN BREASTS

With chicken pieces already cooked, you can do the last minute grilling in no time.

Chicken breasts and thighs, skin removed	6 lbs.	2.75 kg
Ketchup	¹/₂ cup	125 mL
Water	¹/₄ cup	50 mL
Apple juice	¹/₄ cup	50 mL
Lemon juice	2 tbsp.	30 mL
Cider vinegar	1 tbsp.	15 mL
Granulated sugar	2 tbsp.	30 mL
Worcestershire sauce	1 tsp.	5 mL
Seasoned salt	¹/₂ tsp.	2 mL

Cook chicken pieces in covered roaster in 350°F (180°C) oven until barely tender. May be chilled at this point until needed.

In small bowl combine remaining ingredients. Add chicken pieces turning to coat. Let stand 30 minutes. Place chicken pieces on medium-hot grill. Turn and brush with sauce often until glazed. Serves 8.

QUICK CHICKEN: Brush cooked chicken pieces with Barbecue Sauce, page 84, as you heat on grill.

CHICKEN SUPREME IN FOIL

Open these foil packets to chicken in yummy gravy.

Small chicken breasts (or 3 large, halved)	6	6
Condensed cream of mushroom soup	2 x 10 oz.	2 x 284 mL
Chopped green onion	2 tbsp.	30 mL
Parsley flakes	1 tsp.	5 mL
Salt	¹/₂ tsp.	2 mL
Thyme	¹/₄ tsp.	1 mL

Remove skin from chicken. Prepare 6 double thickness foil squares.

Mix soup, onion, parsley, salt and thyme together in bowl. Divide this mixture in half. Spoon ¹/₂ onto center of foil. Place chicken on top. Spoon other half over chicken. Secure foil well. Place on grill over medium heat for about 20 minutes. Turn and cook until tender, about 25 minutes more. Serves 6.

CHICKEN HALVES

Serving is so easy when each person gets half a chicken.

LEMON MARINADE

Lemon juice	$1/3$ cup	75 mL
Cooking oil	$1/4$ cup	50 mL
Worcestershire sauce	1 tbsp.	15 mL
Onion salt	$1/2$ tsp.	2 mL
Celery salt	$1/2$ tsp.	2 mL
Broiler chickens, about 2 lbs. (1.8 kg) each, cut in half	2	2

Lemon Marinade: Combine first 5 ingredients in small bowl.

Brush chicken with marinade. Place flesh side down on grill over medium heat. Turn and baste every 10 minutes until cooked, about $3/4$ to 1 hour. Serves 4.

HONEY CHICKEN

Honey	$1/3$ cup	75 mL
Prepared mustard	1 tbsp.	15 mL
Curry powder	$1/2$ tsp.	2 mL

Mix all ingredients together. Brush over chicken during last stage of cooking.

EASTERN CHICKEN

Marinated in grapefruit juice with lots of extras added.

Grapefruit juice	$1 1/2$ cups	375 mL
Cooking oil	$1/2$ cup	125 mL
Vinegar	$1/4$ cup	50 mL
Granulated sugar	1 tbsp.	15 mL
Salt	1 tsp.	5 mL
Prepared mustard	1 tsp.	5 mL
Onion flakes	2 tsp.	10 mL
Garlic clove, minced	1	1
Oregano	$1/2$ tsp.	2 mL
Paprika	$1/2$ tsp.	2 mL
Thyme	$1/8$ tsp.	0.5 mL
Chicken parts	3 lbs.	1.4 kg

(continued on next page)

In deep bowl combine first 11 ingredients. Mix well.

Add chicken. Marinate all day or overnight in refrigerator. Place chicken on greased grill over moderate heat. Baste and turn often for about 30 to 35 minutes. Serves 4.

DRUMSTICKS

A great way to enhance leftover chicken.

All-purpose flour	$1/3$ cup	75 mL
Salt	1 tsp.	5 mL
Pepper	$1/4$ tsp.	1 mL
Paprika	$1/2$ tsp.	2 mL
Eggs	2	2
Fine dry bread crumbs	$1/3$ cup	75 mL
Grated Parmesan cheese	$1/3$ cup	75 mL
Chicken drumsticks, cooked and chilled	12	12
Butter or margarine, melted	$1/2$ cup	125 mL

Put flour, salt, pepper and paprika into plastic bag. Shake to mix.

Beat eggs in bowl until smooth.

Mix bread crumbs and Parmesan cheese together in shallow dish.

Remove skin from drumsticks. Put 3 or 4 at a time in bag. Shake to coat with flour. Dip into eggs. Roll in cheese mixture covering completely. Place on tray. Chill for 30 minutes.

Brush with melted butter. Cook on greased medium-hot grill. Turn and baste often for about 15 to 20 minutes.

Pictured on page 35.

Paré Pointer

Children certainly do brighten a home. They never turn the lights off.

BARBECUED CHICKEN

Because of precooking, this chicken is moist and tender when finished on the barbecue.

Chicken legs, complete or cut apart	**3 lbs.**	**1.35 kg**
Chicken breasts, halved	**3 lbs.**	**1.35 kg**

Arrange chicken pieces in roaster. Cover and bake in 325°F (160°C) oven for about 1 hour or until almost cooked. Cool for a few minutes. Chill until ready to barbecue.

Brush all chicken with Lemon Basting Sauce. Let stand 30 minutes. Place on medium-hot grill. Brush sauce on top of chicken pieces. Turn in a few minutes and brush sauce on other side. Repeat. Total cooking time about 30 minutes. Serves 8.

LEMON BASTING SAUCE

Lemon juice	**¹/₃ cup**	**75 mL**
Cooking oil	**¹/₃ cup**	**75 mL**
Wine vinegar	**¹/₃ cup**	**75 mL**
Soy sauce	**¹/₂ tsp.**	**2 mL**
Salt	**1 tsp.**	**5 mL**
Pepper	**¹/₄ tsp.**	**1 mL**
Thyme	**¹/₄ tsp.**	**1 mL**

Mix all ingredients together in saucepan. Heat and stir to boiling. Simmer 2 to 3 minutes. Brush on chicken pieces to marinate and as you heat and turn them. Makes about 1 cup (225 mL).

MAKE AHEAD CHICKEN: As the precooked chicken is heating, brush pieces with your favorite barbecue sauce. Turn and baste until sizzling hot. Fast and easy. You also know it is cooked perfectly.

Paré Pointer

Dust is only mud with the juice squeezed out.

CHICKEN DELISH

This has a hint of tomato flavor without tomato color.

Vinegar	1 1/2 cups	375 mL
Tomato paste	5 1/2 oz.	156 mL
Cooking oil	1/2 cup	125 mL
Salt	2 tsp.	10 mL
Onion powder	1/2 tsp.	2 mL
Garlic powder	1/2 tsp.	2 mL
Paprika	1 tsp.	5 mL
Pepper	1/2 tsp.	2 mL
Worcestershire sauce	1 tbsp.	15 mL
Chicken parts, or halves, or quarters	4 1/2 lbs.	2 kg

Combine first 9 ingredients in bowl. Stir well. Pour into plastic bag.

Add chicken. Seal bag. Chill for 3 to 4 hours or overnight. Cook on medium grill, 20 to 30 minutes total time. Additional basting may be done with sauce if desired. Serves 6.

GRILLED CHICKEN WINGS

They are cooked in a foil pan placed right on the grill.

Chicken wings, tips removed	3 lbs.	1.35 kg
Ketchup	2 tbsp.	30 mL
Cider vinegar	2 tbsp.	30 mL
Cooking oil	1 tbsp.	15 mL
Prepared mustard	1 tsp.	15 mL
Salt	3/4 tsp.	4 mL
Pepper	1/4 tsp.	1 mL
Garlic powder	1/4 tsp.	1 mL

Arrange wings in large foil pan.

Mix remaining ingredients together in small bowl. Spread over wings being sure to get some on every piece. Place uncovered pan on indirect grill (see page 149) in medium heat. Close lid. Cook until browned and tender, about 20 minutes. Rotate pan at half-time. Makes about 18 wings. Serves 3 people, 6 wings each. Cut wings apart to serve 8 people, 4 pieces each as an appetizer.

Pictured on page 89.

ORIENTAL CHICKEN WINGS

These win for flavor every time whether as the main course or an appetizer.

Chicken wings	3 lbs.	1.4 kg
Cooking oil		

ORIENTAL SAUCE		
Soy sauce	1/4 cup	50 mL
Brown sugar	2 tbsp.	30 mL
Onion powder	1/8 tsp.	0.5 mL
Garlic powder	1/8 tsp.	0.5 mL
Ginger	1/8 tsp.	0.5 mL

Brush wings with cooking oil. Place on grill over medium heat for about 3 minutes. Turn to cook other side.

Oriental Sauce: Mix all five ingredients together in small bowl. Brush over tender wings. Continue to cook until glazed well. Makes 3 servings of 6 wings each. To use as an appetizer cut wings apart after cooking to serve 8 people, 4 to 5 pieces each.

Pictured on page 89.

SWEET AND SOUR WINGS

Vinegar	1/4 cup	50 mL
Brown sugar, packed	1/2 cup	125 mL
Soy sauce	1 1/2 tsp.	7 mL
Ketchup	1 tsp.	5 mL

Mix all 4 ingredients together. Brush over cooked wings on both sides until glazed and crusty.

Pare Pointer

If you want your family tree traced without it costing you anything just run for public office.

MAY DAY CHICKEN

For a tasty feast, cook these chicken pieces somewhat before basting.

Chili sauce	1 cup	250 mL
Crabapple or apple jelly	³/₄ cup	175 mL
Chicken bouillon powder	2 tsp.	10 mL
Onion powder	¹/₄ tsp.	1 mL
Mustard powder	¹/₄ tsp.	1 mL
Chicken pieces	3 lbs.	1.4 kg

Measure first 5 ingredients into small saucepan. Heat on edge of grill. Stir often.

Place chicken pieces on greased grill over medium heat. Grill for 10 minutes per side. Baste with sauce. Turn. Baste and turn every 4 minutes until cooked, about 30 to 35 minutes total time. Serves 4.

YAKITORI

These chicken kebabs cook very quickly. Great for both an appetizer and main course. The added mushrooms are good.

Soy sauce	¹/₂ cup	125 mL
Sherry (or alcohol-free sherry)	¹/₄ cup	50 mL
Brown sugar	2 tbsp.	30 mL
Ginger	¹/₂ tsp.	2 mL
Garlic powder	¹/₄ tsp.	1 mL
Boneless chicken breasts	2	2
Button mushrooms	24	24
Green onions	8	8

Mix first 5 ingredients together in deep bowl.

Cut chicken into bite size pieces. Mushroom stems can either be removed or left intact. Cut onions into 1 inch (2.5 cm) pieces. Put chicken, mushrooms and onion into soy sauce mixture in bowl. Let stand for 30 minutes. Thread skewers (presoak wooden skewers 30 minutes). Use long skewers for the main course or short ones for appetizers. Cook over hot grill. Turn and baste often with remaining sauce. Total time, about 10 to 15 minutes. Makes 4 main course servings or 8 appetizers.

CHICKEN STIR-FRY

As everyone is sitting around you can whip up this stir-fry. To double, cook two batches. Serve with rice.

Cooking oil	2 tbsp.	30 mL
Chicken or pork, cut in small cubes	1 lb.	454 g
Large onion, chopped	1	1
Fresh bean sprouts	12 oz.	350 g
Thinly sliced celery	2 cups	500 mL
Bamboo shoots, drained and sliced	10 oz.	284 mL
Soy sauce	1 tbsp.	15 mL
Garlic powder	1/8 tsp.	0.5 mL
Salt	1/4 tsp.	1 mL
Pepper	1/4 tsp.	1 mL
Beef bouillon powder	2 tsp.	10 mL
Hot water	1 cup	250 mL
Cornstarch	1 tbsp.	15 mL
Cold water	1 tbsp.	15 mL

Heat cooking oil in wok or large skillet over hot grill. Add chicken. Stir-fry 5 minutes.

Add next 8 ingredients. Stir-fry until chicken has no pink in it and vegetables are tender crisp.

Dissolve beef bouillon in hot water. Add to wok. Stir.

Mix cornstarch in cold water. Add to wok stirring until mixture cooks and thickens. Taste for pepper, adding more as liked. Makes 4 servings.

FAST CHICKEN

Really crusty and delicious.

Soy sauce	1/2 cup	125 mL
Cooking oil	1/4 cup	50 mL
Ketchup	1 tbsp.	15 mL
Garlic powder	1/4 tsp.	1 mL
Chicken pieces	3 lbs.	1.4 kg

Mix soy sauce, cooking oil, ketchup and garlic powder together in small bowl.

Dip chicken pieces in sauce. Place on greased grill over medium heat until cooked on both sides, about 30 minutes total time. Brush with sauce a time or two. Serves 4.

MACARONI SALAD

Good choice for a hot day cookout.

Elbow macaroni (or tiny shells)	2 cups	500 mL
Boiling water	2$\frac{1}{2}$ qts.	3 L
Cooking oil	1 tbsp.	15 mL
Salt	2 tsp.	10 mL
Salad dressing (such as Miracle Whip)	$\frac{3}{4}$ cup	175 mL
Chopped pimiento	2 tbsp.	30 mL
Chopped green onion	2 tbsp.	30 mL
Chopped sweet pickle	2 tbsp.	30 mL
Granulated sugar	1 tbsp.	15 mL
Prepared mustard	1 tsp.	5 mL
Seasoned salt	$\frac{1}{2}$ tsp.	2 mL
Pepper	$\frac{1}{4}$ tsp.	1 mL

Paprika

In large uncovered Dutch oven cook macaroni in boiling water, cooking oil and salt until tender but firm, about 5 to 7 minutes. Drain. Rinse with cold water. Drain well. Return macaroni to pot.

Combine next 8 ingredients in a small bowl. Mix well. Add to macaroni. Toss together well. Turn into serving bowl. Chill for one hour or more. If you want it more moist, add a bit of milk.

Sprinkle with paprika. Makes about 5$\frac{1}{2}$ cups (1.4 L).

Pictured on page 107.

The high cost of living didn't bring them down. It was high living.

CUCUMBER SALAD

A good garden salad when cucumbers are plentiful. May be served any time of year when store bought.

Peeled and cubed cucumbers Salt, sprinkle	4 cups	1 L
Thinly sliced radishes	1/3 cup	75 mL
Sliced green onions	1/4 cup	50 mL
Grated carrot	1/4 cup	50 mL
Mayonnaise	1/2 cup	125 mL
Vinegar	4 tsp.	20 mL
Granulated sugar	2 tsp.	10 mL

Sprinkle cucumber with salt in bowl. Let stand for about 1 hour. Drain.

Add radishes, onion and carrot to cucumber.

In small bowl combine mayonnaise, vinegar and sugar. Stir well. Chill vegetables and dressing separately. Just before serving, drain vegetables well. Pour dressing over vegetables. Toss and serve. Makes 6 servings.

BEAN SPROUT SALAD

This not-so-common salad is excellent. Try something different for a change.

Snow peas, frozen or fresh Boiling salted water	6 oz.	170 g
Fresh bean sprouts	12 oz.	350 g
Grated cabbage, packed	1 cup	250 mL
Chopped pimiento	2 tbsp.	30 mL
DRESSING Salad oil	2 tbsp.	30 mL
Soy sauce	2 tbsp.	30 mL
Vinegar	2 tbsp.	30 mL
Brown sugar	2 tbsp.	30 mL

Cook snow peas in boiling water for 1 minute. Drain. Cool.

Put bean sprouts, cabbage and pimiento into bowl. Add snow peas.

Dressing: Mix all 4 ingredients together in small bowl. Just before serving pour it over vegetables in bowl. Toss to mix. Serves 6.

STUFFED LETTUCE

An appetizing cheese mixture fills the lettuce. Just cut into wedges to serve.

Small heads of lettuce, or 1 large	2	2
Cream cheese, softened	8 oz.	250 g
Grated medium Cheddar cheese	1/2 cup	125 mL
Blue cheese, crumbled	1/4 cup	50 mL
Chopped fresh parsley	2 tbsp.	30 mL
Onion flakes, crushed	2 tsp.	10 mL
Worcestershire sauce	2 tsp.	10 mL

Remove outer leaves of lettuce. Cut out core plus the middle area. Small heads are easier to cut into wedges than large.

Put remaining ingredients in bowl. Mix together well. Stuff into center of lettuce. Wrap in plastic. Chill. To serve cut in wedges. Serve as is or with your favorite dressing. Serves 8 generously.

Pictured on page 107.

COLORFUL COLESLAW

Slivers of red pepper add to both flavor and appearance of this salad. Good.

Finely shredded cabbage, packed	5 cups	1.12 L
Red pepper, slivered	1	1
Grated carrot	1/2 cup	125 mL
Onion flakes	1 tbsp.	15 mL
Parsley flakes	1 tbsp.	15 mL
Salt	1/2 tsp.	2 mL
Celery salt	1/4 tsp.	1 mL
Mayonnaise	1/2 cup	125 mL
Cider vinegar	1 tbsp.	15 mL

In large bowl combine first 7 ingredients. If you prefer to use fresh onion and parsley, use 3 to 4 times as much.

Stir mayonnaise and vinegar together. Add and mix well. Serves 6.

CAESAR SALAD

Still a favorite.

CROUTONS		
White bread slices, cut into cubes and dried to make	2 cups	500 mL
Olive oil, or cooking oil	2 tbsp.	30 mL
Garlic salt, sprinkle (or 1 clove, minced)		

CAESAR DRESSING		
Mayonnaise	1 cup	250 mL
Lemon juice	1 tbsp.	15 mL
Worcestershire sauce	1/2 tsp.	2 mL
Garlic powder	1/4 tsp.	1 mL
Salt	1/4 tsp.	1 mL
Pepper	1/8 tsp.	0.5 mL
Large head of Romaine lettuce	1	1
Grated Parmesan cheese	1/2 cup	125 mL
Prepared croutons		

Croutons: Sauté bread cubes in cooking oil in frying pan. Sprinkle with garlic salt. If using a garlic clove sauté with bread cubes. Stir to brown croutons. Cool.

Caesar Dressing: Mix first 6 ingredients together well in bowl.

Tear or cut lettuce bitesize into large bowl. Add cheese and croutons. When ready to serve pour dressing over top. Toss. Serves 6.

Pictured on page 125.

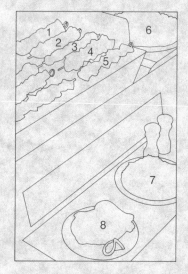

A good salad to have prepared ahead of time.

Medium potatoes	6	6
Boiling salted water		
Diced celery	1 cup	250 mL
Minced onion	2 tbsp.	30 mL
Chopped chives or green onions	2 tbsp.	30 mL
Chopped parsley	1 tsp.	5 mL
Hard boiled eggs, chopped	4	4
Salt	1 tsp.	5 mL
Pepper	1/4 tsp.	1 mL
Salad dressing (such as Miracle Whip)	1 1/2 cups	375 mL
Milk	1/3 cup	75 mL
Prepared mustard	1 tsp.	5 mL
Granulated sugar	1 tsp.	5 mL
Paprika, sprinkle		

Cook potatoes with their skins on in boiling salted water until tender. Drain. Cool slightly. Remove skins. Dice potatoes into large bowl.

Add celery, onion, chives, parsley, eggs, salt and pepper.

In another bowl stir salad dressing, milk, mustard and sugar together until smooth. Pour over potato mixture. Stir from bottom of bowl. Mix well. Chill.

Sprinkle with paprika before serving. Serves 6 people approximately 1 cup (250 mL) each.

Pictured on page 53.

When a hobo comes to your house and knocks on your door it would be a bum rap.

TOSSED SPINACH SALAD

A good outdoor mixture.

Large bunch of spinach leaves (or use Romaine lettuce)	1	1
Small red onion, thinly sliced	1	1
Croutons	1/2 cup	125 mL
Button mushrooms	1 1/2 cups	375 mL
Peeled and chopped cucumber	1 1/2 cups	375 mL
Bacon slices, cooked and crumbled	6	6
Hard-boiled eggs, chopped	2	2
DRESSING		
Cooking oil	1/3 cup	75 mL
Granulated sugar	1/3 cup	75 mL
Ketchup	1/4 cup	60 mL
Vinegar	3 tbsp.	50 mL
Onion flakes	1 1/2 tbsp.	25 mL
Worcestershire sauce	1 1/2 tsp.	7 mL

Put spinach into large bowl. Tear large leaves. Add next 6 ingredients. Chill.

Dressing: Mix all ingredients together in small bowl. Stir well. Cover and chill a few hours ahead if possible. Just before serving, pour dressing over salad. Toss. Serves 8.

TOSSED SALAD

A very full salad. Bound to please everyone.

Head lettuce, cut up	1	1
Sliced fresh mushrooms	1 cup	250 mL
Green onions, sliced	4	4
Radishes, sliced	6	6
Chopped cucumber	1/2 cup	125 mL
Sliced celery	1/2 cup	125 mL
Hard-boiled eggs, chopped	2	2
Tomato, chopped	1	1
DRESSING		
Mayonnaise	1/2 cup	125 mL
Prepared mustard	1 tsp.	5 mL
Granulated sugar	1 tsp.	5 mL
Milk	2 tbsp.	30 mL

(continued on next page)

Combine first 8 ingredients in large bowl. If storing in refrigerator before dressing salad, keep tomato separate until ready to toss as it could go a bit watery.

Dressing: Stir mayonnaise, mustard, sugar and milk together in small bowl. Pour over salad in bowl. Toss and serve. Serves 8.

ONION RING SPECIAL

This can be made a few days ahead. Use as a salad, or to add to a sandwich or to serve as a condiment with meat and hamburgers. Keeps and keeps.

Large onion, sliced in very thin rings	1	1
Cold water to cover		
Red pepper, sliced in rings	1	1
Green pepper, sliced in rings	1	1
Yellow pepper, sliced in rings	1	1
Granulated sugar	1$\frac{1}{3}$ cups	300 mL
Water	1$\frac{1}{3}$ cups	300 mL
Vinegar	1$\frac{1}{3}$ cups	300 mL
Cooking oil	2 tbsp.	30 mL

Use food slicer if possible to get very thin onion slices. Separate slices into rings. Soak in cold water for 1 hour. Drain.

Add pepper rings to onion rings in large container.

Mix sugar, second amount of water, vinegar and cooking oil together in saucepan over medium heat. Bring to a boil. Stir until sugar dissolves. Remove from heat. Pour over onion-pepper mixture. Cover. Chill for at least 24 hours before serving. Serves 10.

Pictured on page 17.

Blood is not only thicker than water but it boils faster too.

GOOD GREEN BEANS

Try all three — Good, Better and Best.

Green beans, cut, fresh or frozen	1 lb.	454 g
Green onions, chopped	2	2
Butter or margarine	1 tbsp.	15 mL
Salt, sprinkle		
Pepper, sprinkle		
Water	4 tbsp.	60 mL

On 4 greased double thickness layers of foil divide beans and onion. Add ¹/₂ tsp. (2 mL) butter and a sprinkle of salt and pepper. Add 1 tbsp. (15 mL) water to each. Wrap. Cook on grill over medium heat for about 20 minutes. Turn occasionally. Makes 4 servings.

BETTER GREEN BEANS: Add ¹/₂ tsp. (2 mL) soy sauce to each packet.

BEST GREEN BEANS: Add ¹/₂ tsp. (2 mL) soy sauce to each packet plus at least 1 tsp. (5 mL) toasted slivered almonds. Toast almonds in 350°F (180°C) oven for 5 to 10 minutes. Stir once or twice.

SWEET POTATOES

A good extra to serve with meat.

**Sweet potatoes, peeled, sliced in oval
   slices ¹/₂-³/₄ inch (12-18 mm) thick
Cooking oil**

Brush potato slices with cooking oil. Cook on grill over medium heat for about 8 to 10 minutes per side. Turn and brush with cooking oil to cook on second side until tender.

YAMS: These have purple-colored skin as compared to the orange skin of sweet potatoes. Cook the same way.

FOILED SWEET POTATOES: Cut into slices ¹/₂ inch to ³/₄ inch (12 to 18 mm) thick. Lay 2 slices side by side on double thickness of foil. Put dabs of butter here and there on potato. Sprinkle with salt and pepper. Wrap. Cook on grill over medium heat about 7 to 8 minutes per side.

TURNIP: Both the white turnip and yellow turnip are very good cooked in foil like Foiled Sweet Potatoes. They will take about 10 to 13 minutes per side.

VEGETABLE PACKETS

A colorful addition to any meal.

Carrots, thinly sliced	1 lb.	454 g
Peas, fresh or frozen	1 lb.	454 g
Fresh mushrooms, thinly sliced	½ lb.	225 g
Butter or margarine	4 tsp.	20 mL
Salt, sprinkle		
Pepper, sprinkle		
Water	6 tbsp.	100 mL

Using 6 double thickness foil squares, divide carrots, peas and mushrooms. Add 1 tsp. (5 mL) butter to each. Sprinkle with salt and pepper. Add 1 tbsp. (15 mL) water to each. Cook over medium-hot grill for a total of about 15 minutes. Turn occasionally. Makes 6 medium servings.

Pictured on page 17.

PEAS AND MUSHROOMS: These go very well together. Just omit the carrots. Cooking time will be about 10 to 15 minutes.

STIR-FRIED VEGETABLES

Stir up a batch of good, easy and colorful vegetables.

Cooking oil	2 tbsp.	30 mL
Medium onions, cut in strips	2	2
Sliced mushrooms	2 cups	500 mL
Frozen peas, thawed	10 oz.	284 g
Cherry tomatoes, quartered	12	12
Salt, sprinkle		
Pepper, sprinkle		

Heat cooking oil in wok or large frying pan on grill over medium-high heat. Add onion. Stir-fry for about 5 minutes.

Add mushrooms. Stir-fry until onion is tender crisp.

Add peas and tomatoes. Stir-fry until hot and peas are cooked.

Sprinkle with salt and pepper. Stir. Serves 6.

PIT CORN ROAST

This corn roast will serve as many as you want it to. There is no limit. Just use more corn and a bigger pit.

Corn cobs, with husks intact
Tub of water

Stones (optional)
Newspaper
Dry kindling
Dry wood

Butter or margarine, melted
  (butter is best)
Salt
Pepper

Paper towels for napkins and
  towel use
Soapy water

This is ideal for a farm. Check fire regulations before beginning.

Place corn cobs into tub of cold water to soak about 1 hour.

Dig a shallow pit about 5 inches (13 cm) deep making it 3 × 8 feet (1 × 2.5 m) ground size. If using stones place around outside edge of pit. Build a huge bonfire in pit. Long logs are easier to stack than short logs.

When flames are gone, work quickly. Rake embers to edges of pit right to the ground lengthwise. Lay wet corn on ground. There can be 2 or 3 layers. Rake embers from sides over top of corn to cover well. Cook for about 20 minutes. Test one to check. Rake back coals.

When corn can be handled let guests remove husks and silk, dip cob into a jar of melted butter and add a sprinkle of salt and pepper if desired. Melted butter may also be in a flatish bowl or pan.

For a corn roast only, be sure to supply drinks and allow approximately 4 cobs per person. You are not responsible for a guest's nutrition at such a feast. However, you can serve other additional food if you like, cutting corn quantity accordingly.

Paper towels are sturdier and preferable to paper napkins. And for those that find themselves with butter up to their elbows a pail of soapy water is a must.

Note: Instead of tubs, clean out plastic garbage pails to soak corn.

MUSHROOMS

These favorites cook fairly quickly and go with anything.

Medium fresh mushrooms	36 - 48	36 - 48
Butter or margarine	6 tbsp.	90 mL
Salt, sprinkle		
Pepper, sprinkle		

On square of foil arrange 6 to 8 mushrooms. Add 1 tbsp. (15 mL) butter. Sprinkle with salt and pepper. Wrap. Repeat for 5 more packets. Cook on medium-hot grill turning once, about 8 minutes total cooking time. Serves 6.

MUSHROOM KEBABS: You will find these excellent when marinated in any marinade used for meat. Thread them onto skewers (presoak wooden skewers 30 minutes) when meat is nearly cooked. Cook mushrooms on grill, turning occasionally until soft.

MUSHROOM PACKETS

Served in sauce in a packet!

Finely chopped onion	¹/₂ cup	125 mL
Butter or margarine	2 tbsp.	30 mL
All-purpose flour	1 tbsp.	15 mL
Salt	¹/₄ tsp.	1 mL
Pepper, light sprinkle		
Paprika	¹/₄ tsp.	1 mL
Chicken bouillon powder	1 tsp.	5 mL
Sour cream	¹/₂ cup	125 mL
Fresh small mushrooms	1 lb.	454 g

Sauté onion in butter in frying pan until clear and soft.

Mix in flour, salt, pepper, paprika and bouillon powder. Stir in sour cream until it boils and thickens. Cool.

On a square of foil place about ¹/₄ of the mushrooms. Spoon ¹/₄ sour cream mixture over top. Wrap. Repeat to make 3 more packets. Cook on medium-hot grill, turning once for about 8 minutes total cooking time. Serves 4.

Paré Pointer

Many anglers insist that fishing is a reel sport.

QUICK ONIONS

Such a good sauce when these packets are opened.

Large onions, peeled	3	3
Boiling salted water		
Corn syrup	$1/_3$ cup	75 mL
Barbecue Sauce, see page 84	$1/_3$ cup	75 mL

Boil whole onions in salted water until tender. Drain well. Cool a bit. Cut each onion in half crosswise.

Mix corn syrup and barbecue sauce together in small bowl. Put each $1/_2$ onion on square of double thickness of foil. Spoon sauce over top, dividing among them. Wrap. Heat on grill, turning often, about 10 minutes total time. Makes 6 servings.

Pictured on page 143.

BARBECUED BABY CORN

Can a vegetable be cute?

Canned baby corn, drained	14 oz.	398 mL
Butter or margarine	$1/_2$ cup	125 mL
Lemon juice	$1/_2$ tsp.	2 mL
Seasoned salt	$1/_4$ tsp.	1 mL
Pepper	$1/_8$ tsp.	0.5 mL

Pat corn dry with paper towels.

Put next 4 ingredients into small saucepan on edge of grill to melt. These are nice on a skewer (presoak wooden skewers 30 minutes) but usually they break apart. Brush cobs with butter mixture. Lay them across grill over medium heat. Cook for about 10 minutes total time. Turn and baste occasionally. Makes 4 servings.

Pictured on page 35.

Pare Pointer

Ask a question in Bengal and you get a Bengal Lancer.

PEPPER STIR-FRY

Peter Piper's peppers at their best.

Cooking oil	2 tbsp.	30 mL
Small red onion, sliced	1	1
Green pepper, cut in strips	2	2
Yellow pepper, cut in strips	2	2
Red pepper, diced	1/2	1/2
Medium zucchini, cut in short fingers	1	1
Bean sprouts, large handful	1	1

Salt, sprinkle
Pepper, sprinkle
Toasted slivered almonds, sprinkle
   (toast in 350°F, 180°C, oven until
   browned, stirring once or twice
   about 5 minutes)

Heat cooking oil in wok or large frying pan on grill. Add onion. Stir-fry for 5 minutes.

Add green, yellow and red peppers. Add zucchini. Stir-fry until tender crisp, about 5 minutes.

Add bean sprouts. Stir-fry until heated through.

Sprinkle with salt and pepper and toasted almonds. Makes 4 servings.

Pictured on page 53.

PEAS AND BACON

Bacon and onion are added for a different and tasty flavor to peas in a packet.

Bacon slices, diced	2	2
Chopped onion	1/4 cup	50 mL
Frozen peas	10 oz.	284 g

Sauté bacon and onion together in frying pan until bacon is cooked. Remove from heat. Cool.

Add peas. Stir. Wrap about 1/4 in double thickness of foil. Repeat to make 3 more packets. Cook on grill over medium-hot heat turning once for 10 to 15 minutes total time. Makes 4 medium servings.

QUICK VEGETABLE PACKETS

Grill these packets to complete your meal.

Sliced carrot	2 cups	500 mL
Corn on the cob, sliced 1 inch (2.5 cm) thick in rounds and then cut in half	2	2
Sliced onion	2 cups	500 mL
Whole green beans, fresh or frozen	10 oz.	284 g
Salt, sprinkle		
Pepper, sprinkle		
Butter or margarine	¼ cup	50 mL
Water	6 tbsp.	100 mL

Divide vegetables onto 4 greased, double thickness squares of foil. Sprinkle with salt and pepper. Dot some butter on each. Add 1 ½ tbsp. (25 mL) water to each packet. Seal. Cook on medium-hot grill until tender, about 15 to 20 minutes. Turn occasionally. Makes 4 servings.

PACKETS WITH CHEESE: When vegetables are cooked open foil. Sprinkle each packet with ½ cup (125 mL) grated medium Cheddar cheese. Close foil. Return to grill to melt cheese. Do not turn.

Pictured on page 143.

BBQ BAKED POTATOES

Serve these with the foil rolled back all prepared for your favorite topping.

Medium size baking potatoes	6	6
Butter or margarine	6 tsp.	30 mL
Salt, sprinkle		
Pepper, sprinkle		
Butter or margarine, softened	½ cup	125 mL
Chopped chives	1 tbsp.	15 mL

Rub potato skins with first amount of butter. Using double thickness of foil wrap each potato snugly. Cook on medium grill, turning once, about 20 minutes on each side. With an oven mitt press potato to see if it is done. It should feel soft when pushed with thumb. Unwrap and make a slit in the top in both directions. Push ends upward to open it.

Sprinkle with salt and pepper.

Mix butter with chives. Put a dollop on top. Serves 6.

Pictured on page 17.

QUICK POTATOES

These are precooked. They warm up very well. With the onion and cheese they taste fresh.

Medium potatoes	6	6
Boiling salted water		
Sliced onion	1 cup	250 mL
Butter or margarine	2 tbsp.	30 mL
Grated medium Cheddar cheese	2 cups	500 mL
(or use 1¹/₂ process cheese slices)		

Cook potatoes in their skins in boiling salted water until barely done. Peel. Cool.

Sauté onion in butter until barely soft. Cool. This and the potatoes can be prepared well ahead of time.

On square of double thickness of greased foil, slice 1 potato. Spread ¹/₆ of the onion over top. Cover with ¹/₃ cup (75 mL) of grated cheese. Wrap. Repeat to make 5 more. Cook on medium-hot grill, turning a few times for about 6 minutes. Makes 6 servings.

FROZEN VEGETABLES

Nothing could be more simple than to place a frozen block of a vegetable on foil to cook.

Frozen vegetables in a block,	10 oz.	284 g
peas, carrots, cauliflower, broccoli		
or any other		
Butter or margarine	2 tsp.	10 mL
Salt, sprinkle		
Pepper, sprinkle		
Water	1 tbsp.	15 mL

Place frozen block of vegetable on greased double thickness foil square. Add butter. Sprinkle with salt, pepper and water. Wrap. Place on medium-hot grill for about 15 minutes total time. Turn occasionally. Makes 4 medium servings.

ASPARAGUS

Enjoy one of the first spring vegetables to appear. It cooks more evenly with thick stalks in one packet and thin in another.

Asparagus	1 lb.	454 g
Butter or margarine	4 tsp.	20 mL
Lemon juice (optional)	4 tsp.	20 mL
Salt, sprinkle		
Pepper, sprinkle		
Mock Hollandaise Sauce, page 83 (optional)		

Cut off tough stem ends of asparagus. Divide stalks among 4 double thickness greased foil squares. Add 1 tsp. (5 mL) each of butter and lemon juice to each one. Sprinkle with salt and pepper. Wrap. Cook on grill over medium-hot heat for about 15 to 20 minutes. Turn occasionally.

Pour Mock Hollandaise Sauce over top or serve as is. Makes 4 servings.

CHEEZY ASPARAGUS: Add at least 2 tbsp. (30 mL) grated medium Cheddar cheese to each packet.

ASPARAGUS PARMESAN: Add about 1 tsp. (5 mL) grated Parmesan cheese to each packet.

SESAME ASPARAGUS: Add at least ¹/₂ tsp. (2 mL) toasted sesame seeds to each packet.

CORN ON THE COB

Grilling corn this way there are no husks or silk to contend with. You will enjoy the touch of soy sauce.

Corn cobs	6	6
Butter or margarine, softened	6 tbsp.	100 mL
Soy sauce	2 tsp.	10 mL

Remove husks and silk from corn cobs.

Mix butter and soy sauce together. Spread over corn. Wrap each cob in double thickness of foil. Cook on grill, turning ¹/₄ turn every 3 minutes. Makes 6 servings.

NEW CARROTS

Colorful for any meal combination.

Small carrots, or larger ones, cut	1 lb.	454 g
Butter or margarine	4 tsp.	20 mL
Salt, sprinkle		
Pepper, sprinkle		
Water (optional)	4 tsp.	20 mL

Divide carrots among 4 double thickness squares of foil. Add 1 tsp. (5 mL) butter to each packet and sprinkle with salt and pepper. If carrots have water clinging to them you don't need to add any. If they don't, add 1 tsp. (5 mL) water to each packet. Wrap securely. Cook on grill over medium heat turning occasionally for a total time of about 25 minutes. Serves 4.

QUICK CORN

Delectable! Corn may be soaked or not before grilling. Try both ways. Both work well.

Corn cobs	6	6
Butter or margarine		
Salt, sprinkle		
Pepper, sprinkle		

Pull husks down to the end of cob being careful not to pull them off. Remove silk. Spread corn with butter. Sprinkle with salt and pepper. Bring husks up to cover entire ear. Use pieces of fine wire to secure in 3 or 4 places. If husks cover well no wire is needed.

Cook on grill turning $1/4$ turn each time, allowing about 3 minutes cooking each turn. Remove wire and husks to serve. Makes 6 servings.

CORN IN FOIL: Peeled cob may be wrapped in foil to cook. Brush with butter or margarine before wrapping.

HUSKY CORN: Leave husks intact and cook on grill. Don't peel back husks to remove silk. Add butter, salt and pepper after cooking. This is the easiest and works well.

Pictured on cover.

POTATO EXPRESS

The tops of these potatoes are tops in taste. The best.

Medium size baking potatoes	6	6
Butter or margarine		
Cream cheese, softened	4 oz.	125 g
Sour cream	1/2 cup	125 mL
Onion salt	1 1/2 tsp.	7 mL
Pepper	1/8 tsp.	0.5 mL

Rub potato skins with butter. Wrap each potato tightly in a square of double thickness of foil. Cook on medium grill, turning once for about 20 minutes per side. With an oven mitt press potato to see if it's done. It should feel soft when pushed with thumb. Open foil. Cut top of potato in both directions. Push up on ends to break open.

Beat remaining ingredients together. Spoon dollop over each potato. Serve 6.

POTATO TOPPING: Mix 1 cup (250 mL) sour cream and 1 tsp. (5 mL) onion salt together. Add a few chives or parsley flakes for color. Spoon onto potatoes.

TOMATO ZUCCHINI PARCELS

Moist and colorful.

Zucchini, about 1 1/4 inch (3 cm) diameter, with skin	2	2
Tomatoes, peeled	3	3
Basil	1/2 tsp.	2 mL
Salt, sprinkle		
Pepper, sprinkle		

Cut zucchini into 1 inch (2.5 cm) slices. Dip tomatoes into boiling water for 1 minute or so until they peel easily. Peel and cut into 4 wedges each. Divide zucchini and tomato among 4 double thickness squares of foil. Sprinkle each with 1/8 tsp. (0.5 mL) basil and a sprinkle of salt and pepper. Wrap. Cook over medium-hot grill for a total time of 20 to 25 minutes. Turn occasionally. Serves 4.

POTATO PATTIES

Use leftover potatoes or start from scratch.

Medium potatoes, with peel	4	4
Boiling salted water		
Sliced green onion	¹/₄ cup	50 mL
Salt, sprinkle		
Pepper, sprinkle		
Butter or margarine, melted	¹/₄ cup	50 mL

Cook potatoes in boiling salted water until barely tender. Drain. Cool until you can hold one. Peel. Grate on medium grater.

Add green onion. Sprinkle with salt and pepper. Mix well. Shape into 4 patties. Flour your hands once in awhile if needed. Place in greased wire hamburger basket. Grill over moderate heat about 7 minutes per side.

Brush with butter occasionally. Makes 4 servings.

Pictured on page 143.

BAKED POTATOES: Wrap potatoes in foil. Bake in oven. Take outside to barbecue and place on side or on warming shelf.

POTATO KEBABS

It is best to precook new little potatoes as they most often break when raw and pierced with a skewer. Now this is a treat.

Small new potatoes	18	18
Boiling salted water		
Butter or margarine, melted	¹/₄ cup	50 mL
Dill weed	¹/₂ tsp.	2 mL

Cook potatoes in their skins in boiling salted water until just barely tender. Drain. Set aside until ready to finish.

Thread potatoes on skewers (presoak wooden skewers 30 minutes). Mix melted butter and dill weed together and brush potatoes. Cook on greased grill over medium-hot heat. Turn and baste frequently until they are heated through, about 4 minutes. Serves 6 people, allowing 3 potatoes each.

Variation: Use sour cream instead of butter. Add dill weed and brush potatoes.

PINEAPPLE BEANS

If you haven't tried this combination you are in for a treat. The addition of bacon is also a plus in flavor.

Bacon slices	6	6
Chopped onion	1$\frac{1}{2}$ cups	325 mL
Baked beans in tomato sauce	2 x 14 oz.	2 x 398 mL
Chili sauce	2 tbsp.	30 mL
Molasses	1 tbsp.	15 mL
Prepared mustard	1 tsp.	5 mL
Crushed pineapple, drained	14 oz.	398 mL
Salt	$\frac{1}{4}$ tsp.	1 mL
Pepper	$\frac{1}{8}$ tsp.	0.5 mL

In large saucepan sauté bacon and onion together until cooked. Drain and discard fat.

Add remaining ingredients. Bring to a boil. Cover and simmer for 30 minutes or more. This may be done on the stove and set on the edge of the grill or it can be cooked the whole time on the grill. Makes 8 servings.

Pictured on page 17.

1. Quick Vegetable Packets page 136
2. Quick Onions page 134
3. Potato Patties page 141
4. Sour Milk Quickbread page 47
5. Bran Bread page 52
6. Trout In A Basket page 67

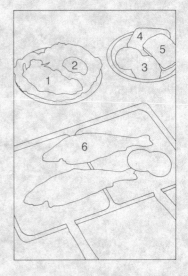

PEPPER PICKINGS

Very showy and lively.

Green peppers, cut in 1 inch (2.5 cm) squares	2	2
Red peppers, cut in 1 inch (2.5 cm) squares	2	2
Yellow peppers, cut in 1 inch (2.5 cm) squares	2	2
Cooking oil	1/3 cup	75 mL
Garlic salt, sprinkle		
Pepper, sprinkle		

Thread 4 green, red and yellow pepper squares on each skewer (presoak wooden skewers 30 minutes) arranging in alternate colors.

Brush with cooking oil. Cook on greased medium grill turning and basting every minute or so until peppers begin to char, about 8 to 10 minutes.

Sprinkle with garlic salt and pepper. Serves 4.

CRUMBED TOMATOES

A cheery-looking vegetable that cooks quickly.

Large tomatoes	3	3
Butter or margarine	3 tbsp.	50 mL
Dry bread crumbs	1/3 cup	75 mL
Grated medium Cheddar cheese	1/4 cup	50 mL
Granulated sugar	1/2 tsp.	2 mL
Basil	1/4 tsp.	1 mL
Salt	1/4 tsp.	1 mL
Pepper, sprinkle		

Cut tomatoes in half crosswise. Gently squeeze out seeds and juice.

Melt butter in small saucepan. Remove from heat. Add remaining ingredients. Mix well. Spoon into tomato halves. Put tomatoes into pan on grill over moderate heat. Close lid. Cook for 5 to 10 minutes until tender. Makes 6 servings.

BAKED ONIONS

Open these packets to onion in a creamy sauce.

Onions, peeled and cut in small wedges	1 lb.	454 g
Butter or margarine	4 tsp.	20 mL
Salt, sprinkle		
Pepper, sprinkle		
Condensed cream of mushroom soup	10 oz.	284 mL

Divide onion among 4 double thickness foil squares. Add 1 tsp. (5 mL) butter to each. Sprinkle with salt and pepper. Add about 4 tbsp. (60 mL) of soup to each. Wrap. Cook on medium grill for about 20 to 25 minutes total. Turn occasionally. Serves 4.

BEANS ON THE BARBECUE

You can heat these on the stove or on the barbecue. They require only a short preparation time. Easy to double.

Butter or margarine	2 tbsp.	30 mL
Chopped onion	1 cup	250 mL
Baked beans in tomato sauce	14 oz.	398 mL
Brown sugar, packed	1/3 cup	75 mL
Ketchup	3 tbsp.	50 mL
Worcestershire sauce	2 tbsp.	30 mL
Prepared mustard	1 tsp.	5 mL

Melt butter in large saucepan. Add onion. Sauté until clear and soft.

Add remaining ingredients. Stir. Bring to a boil. Simmer for 10 minutes. Place on side of barbecue grill to keep hot. Stir occasionally. Serves 4.

Pare Pointer

Hasn't she got a lot of drive? She goes forward by patting herself on the back.

STUFFED PEPPERS

A pepper makes a tasty edible container for rice. Red and yellow peppers may also be used.

Green peppers, or use red	4	4
Boiling salted water		
Cooked long grain rice	3 cups	675 mL
(1½ cups, 350 mL, raw)		
Chopped pimiento	1 tbsp.	15 mL
Condensed cream of mushroom soup	10 oz.	284 mL
Butter or margarine	1 tbsp.	15 mL
Dry bread crumbs	4 tbsp.	60 mL

Choose green peppers that will stand without tipping over easily. Short fat ones are good. Cut off tops. Remove seeds. Cook in boiling salted water for 8 minutes. Drain well. Cool.

Mix rice, pimiento and mushroom soup together in bowl. Stuff peppers.

Melt butter in small saucepan. Stir in bread crumbs until combined. Divide among tops of peppers. Cook on indirect moderate heat in closed barbecue (see page 149), about 30 minutes.

ROAST POTATOES

An easy way to have browned roasted potatoes.

Medium potatoes	6	6
Boiling salted water		
Cooking oil or butter or margarine		

Cook potatoes in their jackets in boiling salted water for about 30 minutes until they are almost done. Use a sharp knife rather than a fork to test for doneness. Cool a bit until you can handle them. Peel. Leave whole or cut in half crosswise.

Brush with cooking oil or butter. Heat on medium-hot grill turning and basting occasionally until browned and crusted. Total time is about 15 to 20 minutes.

BRUSSELS SPROUTS

With or without sauce these are great. So easy.

Frozen Brussels sprouts	10 oz.	284 g
Butter or margarine	2 tbsp.	30 mL
Water	1 tbsp.	15 mL
Lemon juice	$1/2$ tsp.	2 mL
Salt, sprinkle		
Pepper, sprinkle		

Put Brussels sprouts on double thickness sheet of foil. Divide butter over top in pieces. Add water, lemon juice, salt and pepper. Wrap. Cook on grill over medium heat, about 5 to 7 minutes per side. Makes 4 servings.

BRUSSELS SPROUTS IN SAUCE: Lay Brussels sprouts on double thickness foil square. Spoon a 10 oz. (284 mL) can of condensed cream of mushroom soup over top. Wrap. Cook on grill over medium heat about 5 to 7 minutes per side. Makes 4 servings.

PEPPER AND TATER KEBABS

With potatoes prepared ahead this colorful skewer can be ready in a jiffy.

Potatoes with peel, cut in chunks	4	4
Boiling salted water		
Red pepper, cut in squares	1	1
Green pepper, cut in squares	1	1
Yellow pepper, cut in squares	1	1
Butter or margarine, melted	$1/4$ cup	50 mL

Cook potatoes in boiling salted water until tender crisp. Drain. Cool until you can handle them.

Thread skewers (presoak wooden skewers 30 minutes) with potato and peppers, alternating colors.

Brush with melted butter. Cook on grill over medium heat for about 10 minutes until peppers show signs of charring. Turn and baste occasionally. Serves 4.

Pictured on cover.

Both quick and colorful.

Zucchini chunks with peel	12	12
Cherry tomatoes	12	12
Mushrooms	12	12
Italian dressing		

Put vegetables on 4 skewers (presoak wooden skewers 30 minutes) alternating vegetables as you do so.

Brush with Italian dressing. Let stand for 15 minutes. Cook on grill over medium heat. Turn and brush with Italian dressing often. Cook for about 5 minutes until tender and crisp. Makes 4 servings.

INDIRECT COOKING

The Indirect Cooking method is used for anything normally cooked in an oven, such as: pie, cake, biscuits, bread, quickbread and yorkshire pudding, as well as meat and poultry.

If using a gas barbecue with two burners, turn on only one burner. To bake a pie or cake ensure temperature is correct first. Place an oven thermometer over unlit burner in closed barbecue. When temperature is reached, put item to be baked on grill over unlit burner. Bake with lid closed. To cook meat, set drip tray beneath meat on unlit side of grill. No water is necessary in drip pan. Cook with the lid down. Check temperature with oven thermometer so the heat can be regulated.

For baking or cooking meat on a charcoal barbecue, push the coals to one side and bake or cook over the other side. Keep the lid down. Be sure to put a drip pan on the floor of the barbecue underneath the meat.

The lowest flame should give medium heat in a closed barbecue. A medium flame should give high heat.

Paré Pointer

The best dressed insect is a flea. It's always in a fur coat.

MEASUREMENT TABLES

Throughout this book measurements are given in Conventional and Metric measure. To compensate for differences between the two measurements due to rounding, a full metric measure is not always used. The cup used is the standard 8 fluid ounce. Temperature is given in degrees Fahrenheit and Celsius. Baking pan measurements are in inches and centimetres as well as quarts and litres. An exact metric conversion is given below as well as the working equivalent (Standard Measure).

OVEN TEMPERATURES

Fahrenheit (°F)	Celsius (°C)
175°	80°
200°	95°
225°	110°
250°	120°
275°	140°
300°	150°
325°	160°
350°	175°
375°	190°
400°	205°
425°	220°
450°	230°
475°	240°
500°	260°

SPOONS

Conventional Measure	Metric Exact Conversion Millilitre (mL)	Metric Standard Measure Millilitre (mL)
1/8 teaspoon (tsp.)	0.6 mL	0.5 mL
1/4 teaspoon (tsp.)	1.2 mL	1 mL
1/2 teaspoon (tsp.)	2.4 mL	2 mL
1 teaspoon (tsp.)	4.7 mL	5 mL
2 teaspoons (tsp.)	9.4 mL	10 mL
1 tablespoon (tbsp.)	14.2 mL	15 mL

CUPS

	Metric Exact Conversion	Metric Standard Measure
1/4 cup (4 tbsp.)	56.8 mL	60 mL
1/3 cup (5 1/3 tbsp.)	75.6 mL	75 mL
1/2 cup (8 tbsp.)	113.7 mL	125 mL
2/3 cup (10 2/3 tbsp.)	151.2 mL	150 mL
3/4 cup (12 tbsp.)	170.5 mL	175 mL
1 cup (16 tbsp.)	227.3 mL	250 mL
4 1/2 cups	1022.9 mL	1000 mL (1 L)

PANS

Conventional Inches	Metric Centimetres
8x8 inch	20x20 cm
9x9 inch	22x22 cm
9x13 inch	22x33 cm
10x15 inch	25x38 cm
11x17 inch	28x43 cm
8x2 inch round	20x5 cm
9x2 inch round	22x5 cm
10x4 1/2 inch tube	25x11 cm
8x4x3 inch loaf	20x10x7 cm
9x5x3 inch loaf	22x12x7 cm

DRY MEASUREMENTS

Conventional Measure Ounces (oz.)	Metric Exact Conversion Grams (g)	Metric Standard Measure Grams (g)
1 oz.	28.3 g	30 g
2 oz.	56.7 g	55 g
3 oz.	85.0 g	85 g
4 oz.	113.4 g	125 g
5 oz.	141.7 g	140 g
6 oz.	170.1 g	170 g
7 oz.	198.4 g	200 g
8 oz.	226.8 g	250 g
16 oz.	453.6 g	500 g
32 oz.	907.2 g	1000 g (1 kg)

CASSEROLES (Canada & Britain)

Standard Size Casserole	Exact Metric Measure
1 qt. (5 cups)	1.13 L
1 1/2 qts. (7 1/2 cups)	1.69 L
2 qts. (10 cups)	2.25 L
2 1/2 qts. (12 1/2 cups)	2.81 L
3 qts. (15 cups)	3.38 L
4 qts. (20 cups)	4.5 L
5 qts. (25 cups)	5.63 L

CASSEROLES (United States)

Standard Size Casserole	Exact Metric Measure
1 qt. (4 cups)	900 mL
1 1/2 qts. (6 cups)	1.35 L
2 qts. (8 cups)	1.8 L
2 1/2 qts. (10 cups)	2.25 L
3 qts. (12 cups)	2.7 L
4 qts. (16 cups)	3.6 L
5 qts. (20 cups)	4.5 L

INDEX

MAIL ORDER FORM

Deduct $5.00 for every $35.00 ordered

Save $5.00

COMPANY'S COMING SERIES

Quantity		Quantity		Quantity	
	150 Delicious Squares		Main Courses		Light Casseroles
	Casseroles		Pasta		Chicken, Etc.
	Muffins & More		Cakes		Kids Cooking
	Salads		Barbecues		Fish & Seafood
	Appetizers		Dinners of the World		Breads
	Desserts		Lunches		Meatless Cooking
	Soups & Sandwiches		Pies		NEW Cooking For Two (September 1997)
	Holiday Entertaining		Light Recipes		
	Cookies		Microwave Cooking		
	Vegetables		Preserves		

ENGLISH

	NO. OF BOOKS	PRICE
FIRST BOOK: $12.99 + $3.00 shipping = **$15.99 each** x		= $
ADDITIONAL BOOKS: $12.99 + $1.50 shipping = **$14.49 each** x		= $

PINT SIZE BOOKS

Quantity		Quantity		Quantity	
	Finger Food		Buffets		Chocolate
	Party Planning		Baking Delights		NEW Beverages (October 1997)

	NO. OF BOOKS	PRICE
FIRST BOOK: $4.99 + $2.00 shipping = **$6.99 each** x		= $
ADDITIONAL BOOKS: $4.99 + $1.00 shipping = **$5.99 each** x		= $

JEAN PARÉ LIVRES DE CUISINE

Quantity		Quantity		Quantity	
	150 délicieux carrés		Les salades		Les pains
	Les casseroles		La cuisson au micro-ondes		La cuisine sans viande
	Muffins et plus		Les pâtes		NEW La cuisine pour deux (septembre 1997)
	Les dîners		Les conserves		
	Les barbecues		Les casseroles légères		
	Les tartes		Poulet, etc.		
	Délices des fêtes		La cuisine pour les enfants		
	Recettes légères		Poissons et fruits de mer		

FRENCH

	NO. OF BOOKS	PRICE
FIRST BOOK: $12.99 + $3.00 shipping = **$15.99 each** x		= $
ADDITIONAL BOOKS: $12.99 + $1.50 shipping = **$14.49 each** x		= $

TOTAL

- **MAKE CHEQUE OR MONEY ORDER PAYABLE TO:** *COMPANY'S COMING PUBLISHING LIMITED*
- **ORDERS OUTSIDE CANADA:** *Must be paid in U.S. funds by cheque or money order drawn on Canadian or U.S. bank.*
- *Prices subject to change without prior notice.*
- *Sorry, no C.O.D.'s*

TOTAL PRICE FOR ALL BOOKS	$
Less $5.00 for every $35.00 ordered −	$
SUBTOTAL	$
Canadian residents add G.S.T. +	$
TOTAL AMOUNT ENCLOSED	$

Please complete shipping address on reverse.

Gift Giving

- Let us help you with your gift giving!

- We will send cookbooks directly to the recipients of your choice if you give us their names and addresses.

- Be sure to specify the titles you wish to send to each person.

- If you would like to include your personal note or card, we will be pleased to enclose it with your gift order.

- Company's Coming Cookbooks make excellent gifts. Birthdays, bridal showers, Mother's Day, Father's Day, graduation or any occasion... collect them all!

Shipping address

Send the Company's Coming Cookbooks listed on the reverse side of this coupon, to:

Name:

Street:

City: Province/State:

Postal Code/Zip: Tel: (   )   —

Company's Coming Publishing Limited
Box 8037, Station F
Edmonton, Alberta, Canada T6H 4N9
Tel: (403) 450-6223
Fax: (403) 450-1857

Complete your collection.

Look for these *Best-Sellers* where you shop!

COMPANY'S COMING SERIES
Suggested Retail $12.99 each

- ☐ 150 DELICIOUS SQUARES
- ☐ CASSEROLES
- ☐ MUFFINS & MORE
- ☐ SALADS
- ☐ APPETIZERS
- ☐ DESSERTS
- ☐ SOUPS & SANDWICHES
- ☐ HOLIDAY ENTERTAINING
- ☐ COOKIES
- ☐ VEGETABLES
- ☐ MAIN COURSES
- ☐ PASTA
- ☐ CAKES
- ☐ BARBECUES
- ☐ DINNERS OF THE WORLD
- ☐ LUNCHES
- ☐ PIES
- ☐ LIGHT RECIPES
- ☐ MICROWAVE COOKING
- ☐ PRESERVES
- ☐ LIGHT CASSEROLES
- ☐ CHICKEN, ETC.
- ☐ KIDS COOKING
- ☐ FISH & SEAFOOD
- ☐ BREADS
- ☐ MEATLESS COOKING
- ☐ COOKING FOR TWO (September 1997)

PINT SIZE BOOKS
Suggested Retail $4.99 each

- ☐ FINGER FOOD
- ☐ PARTY PLANNING
- ☐ BUFFETS
- ☐ BAKING DELIGHTS
- ☐ CHOCOLATE

All New Recipes

COQ AU VIN

This excellent variation is out of the ordinary to be sure.

Hard margarine (butter browns too fast)	1 tbsp.	15 mL
Chicken parts, skin (removed)	4-5	4-5
All-purpose flour	¼ cup	60 mL
Sliced onion	½ cup	125 mL
Canned tomatoes, mashed	14 oz.	398 mL
Canned whole mushrooms, drained	10 oz.	284 mL
Bay leaf	1	1
Garlic powder	⅛ tsp.	0.5 mL
Granulated sugar	¼ tsp.	1 mL
Salt, sprinkle		
Pepper, sprinkle		
Red wine (or alcohol-free wine)	¼ cup	60 mL

Melt margarine in frying pan. Dip chicken in flour. Brown both sides of chicken in frying pan. Transfer to ungreased 1½ quart (1.5 L) casserole.

Add onion to frying pan. Sauté until browned.

Add next 7 ingredients to onion. Stir. Cook slowly for 5 minutes. Discard bay leaf.

Stir in wine. Pour over chicken. Cover. Bake in 325°F (160°C) oven for 1 to 1½ hours until tender. Serves 2.

Use this handy checklist to complete your collection of
Company's Coming Cookbooks